THE WATER IS STILL WET!

A PADDLER'S GUIDE TO THE STREAMS AND LAKES OF THE BLACK HILLS

EDITED BY: J. KELLY LANE

A Collaborative Effort of
The Black Hills Paddlers

ABOUT THE TITLE

Paddle guide editor Kelly Lane is a long-time area science teacher. Now retired from the classroom, he continues to work with new and young paddlers. Every year Kelly's science classes took a series of field trips to collect water quality data from a local stream. Spring weather in the Black Hills is often less than ideal, in which case students would invariably ask, "Will our field trip be cancelled for weather?" Kelly would answer, "Is the water still wet?" The question was seldom asked again and the field trip was never cancelled. This mantra lives on today; the Black Hills Paddlers also believe that any day is a good day for boating because, "The water is still wet!"

CONTENTS

ACKNOWLEDGMENTS

Thank you to everybody who has helped and contributed but especially to:

- My wife Becky for the total support package, as expected, and so appreciated
- Daughters Ingrid and especially Kelsey, for all the editing
- Mike Ray for wheeling me around and massive whitewater expertise
- Justin Herreman for tireless encouragement and doing the layout
- Chad Andrew for wheels, teaching, beers and wings!
- Dan Crain & Todd Andrew for the ultimate in mentorship
- Nancy Smidt for editing and lake expertise
- Scotty Nelson for boldly writing up routes no one has ever done
- Kevin Eilbeck & April Gregory for the wonderful photography
- Leroy Henderson for Red Water expertise
- Ben Ten Eyck for amazing photos of Spearfish Creek
- Rick Emerson for editing, layout, and more
- Paulette Kirby for "understanding" the pain
- Patrick Fleming for "wheels" on the Cheyenne
- Andrea Story for checking the "rock" gauge at Cascade Springs Bridge
- All The Black Hills Paddlers for staying on me!

DISCLAIMER

River sports are inherently hazardous, involving potential risks that include loss of equipment, injury or death. You are responsible for your own safety, and you assume all risk for your actions. This book does not constitute a recommendation for any person to run any river, and it is no substitute for experience, skill, prudence, common sense, and first-hand observation.

We have tried to make this book as accurate as possible; however, there will inevitably be mistakes and omissions regarding the location, rating, or description of rapids or other features. Our river descriptions do not point out every rapid or hazard. Whitewater difficulty ratings for rivers and rapids are inherently imprecise and subjective. The authors have not run or seen every river in this guide; some of our information, though based on the best available sources both written and oral, is second-hand.

Rivers and rapids are constantly changing, so descriptions that were accurate when they were written may no longer be correct when you run the river. Fluctuations in water levels can dramatically alter the difficulty of any river or rapid. In addition, obstacles and hazards like rocks, falls and logs can and will shift and change from year to year. New dangers may arise or develop at any time. Be prepared. Always trust your own eyes and your own judgment first and foremost. Scout carefully before running any river or rapid, and seek additional advice and information from people who have recently boated the river you are considering.

Boaters should not rely exclusively on the information contained in this book; they should consult local river runners, and government agencies. For more information on river safety, refer to the American Canoe Association website.

We do not guarantee the accuracy of information on land ownership and public access. When in doubt about land ownership and legal access, inquire locally. Nothing we say should be construed as an invitation to trespass.

The authors, editors, publisher, and Black Hills Paddlers Inc. assume no responsibility or liability whatsoever with respect to personal injury, property damage, loss of time or money, or any other loss or damage caused directly or indirectly by the information contained in this book."

Paddle Safe, Paddle Often!

PADDLING THE BLACK HILLS

The Black Hills of South Dakota are virtually unknown as a paddling destination. We often call the Black Hills an "island in the prairie." It is a small, 100-mile square outcrop in an otherwise unforgiving ocean of prairie. So, if we are an "island", there must be some water, right?

There is, although the amount is highly variable. The entire Black Hills drains into the Cheyenne River, via its own headwaters, and tributaries. Most of the waterways out of the Black Hills have multiple man-made dams for flood control, irrigation and recreation.

One little nugget of trivia about this "island in the prairie;" there are no natural lakes in the Black Hills. On the surrounding prairie, five small lakes (without dams) are part of the Cheyenne River drainage. Before human development, all the water flowing out of the Black Hills would wash out to rejuvenate the surrounding prairie and recharge the Madison Aquifer below. Regardless of how you feel about dams, the resulting lakes are a good source of fun for recreation, including recreational and flat water boaters. What about paddling those artificial lakes and the creeks rushing out of the Black Hills? They have been a well-kept secret, known only to a few dedicated locals, and now to YOU!

There are 35 lakes and 33 paddle routes for moving water described in this guide. Black Hills Paddlers have carefully scouted and documented each of the 35 lakes and 33 moving water routes. Members of the group have paddled 30 of the 35 lakes and each of the 33 river and stream routes, most many times!

The South Dakota Canoe & Kayak Association (SDCKA) is the only other formally organized paddler's organization in the state as of 2013. The SDCA centers out of Sioux Falls, which is the population center of our state. There are pockets of paddlers all over the state, though. Notable is the organized group in the Sioux Falls area, and less organized but equally dedicated groups in Pierre, Aberdeen and the Black Hills Paddlers on the Western side of the state. Many boaters talk to each other through websites, blogs or social media. There are more paddlers out there than most of us realize. Read on for background and information on a wealth of places in the Hills where you can whet your appetite to safely "wet a hull."

WHY A PADDLE GUIDE: EDITOR'S NOTE

The Black Hills Paddlers decided to write a paddling guide for two reasons. First, to honor the memory of two pioneering Black Hills paddlers who died in boating accidents on the water they loved. Dan Crain and Todd Andrew were expert boaters. Those of us they mentored in the Black Hills paddling community will always remember Dan and Todd. These two made multiple first descents and started a whole generation of us paddling creeks. The Black Hills Paddlers are committed to helping Todd's brother (ACA certified instructor Chad Andrew) carry on Todd and Dan's work teaching new generations of boaters the joys of safe paddling.

Second and even more personally, I decided to edit this guide as a tool to promote safe boating in my native Black Hills. In 50 years of paddling the Black Hills I have seen and done just about every stupid thing you could imagine. I must have thought I was immortal. But, as the saying goes, "God loves fools and Irishmen, so I am twice blessed." Eighteen years of Parkinson's disease chipped away at the brick veneer I hid my mortality behind.

A couple of years ago that entire brick veneer came crashing down when I had a near-death experience in Rapid Creek. I now understand why trauma can be so terrifying to survivors and rescuers alike. This experience made me rethink my own approach to paddling. I had already lost two friends to freaky whitewater accidents, each man a many-times better paddler than I would ever be. How could I have subjected my current paddle friends to the anguish of dragging what they feared was a dead body out of the water? Many paddlers have quit the water following such a trauma. How dare I give lip service to safety, and then paddle beyond my current limitations!

In follow-up assessment of this accident, we determined that, while we had the right skills and the right gear, poop still happens! The group was physically competent, but mentally blinded. With the peculiarities of Parkinson's, I was a different person every few hours as I took an ever increasing amount of drugs with decreasing efficacy. I was now confronted head on with the cold, deadly reality of play hard, but play safe! While all six of us who paddled that day share some responsibility for the risk my now obvious weakness created, I was the one who insisted on bulling through on the strength of my past. It seems I had left on shore that one most vital piece of safety gear: common sense! This experience and near tragedy has led me to work with the Black Hills Paddlers in creating this guide about paddling Black Hills lakes and streams.

OUR FEARLESS EDITOR KELLY LANE

SAFETY WHEN PADDLING
BLACK HILLS LAKES

- If you're not prepared, stay out of the water!
- Engage your brain "before" getting on the water.
- Never paddle alone!
- If ANYONE in your group is uncomfortable with conditions on the lake stay off the water.
- Paddlers love a beer or a drink, AFTER paddling! They know impaired judgment is an open invite for bad decisions on the water with potentially disastrous consequences!
- Know your route's hazards: If you haven't paddled the lake before, do some homework. What is estimated time paddling, known problems?
- Ask a local for guidance and advice. Members of Black Hills Paddlers will gladly show you our favorite lakes, and probably even come paddle with you.
- Be sure to respect private property and boating regulations. Good habits and a good reputation go a long way when trouble happens and you need a local hand.
- Cold water affects your motor skills, coordination and JUDGEMENT even when air temps are in the 80's.
- Have and practice the skills, knowledge and experience to SAFELY handle wind and hazards before paddling anywhere.
- Have and know how to use proper safety gear.
- We assume that you have left word of your destination and expected return with someone responsible. Don't label yourself with the first three letters of the word when you assume nothing can go wrong, even close to home.
- Lessons from a qualified instructor are a great idea to help you paddle safely. Chad Andrew, ACA certified instructor, offers a wide range of classes for all skill levels.

Remember: ENGAGE YOUR BRAIN

BEFORE ENGAGING THE WATER!!

LAKE PADDLING ETIQUETTE AND THE LAW

Whether you are a grizzled old flat water racer or brand new lake paddler please remember; we do not paddle in a vacuum. Engage your brain before paddling! Traditionally, boaters have been allowed to paddle any water that flows out of the Black Hills.

- There are no natural lakes in the Black Hills, they are all dam created. Somebody paid for that dam! If it is private, stay off the lake without permission! All public accessible lakes in and around the Black Hills and South Dakota are clearly signed. A good rule of thumb: if GFP stocks it with fish it should be public- accessible, possibly with conditions (like the Boy Scout Camp/Medicine Mountain Ranch.)
- Pack out what you pack in! Leave no trace.
- Respect other recreational users on the water.
- Parking for lakes. For-crying out loud, pay the parking/user fee! A SD State Parks annual entrance license is a bargain for all the services you get. The Black Hills National Forest annual recreational user pass is also a bargain. Refer to the pages on Entrance Fees/ User Fees for details. With a permit or permission you won't get hassled; you won't get nasty notes on your car windshield. You've got a nice boat and nice gear, now pay to play!

REQUIRED EQUIPMENT

As responsible paddlers, we already paddle with more safety gear than required by law. South Dakota Law requires:

1. Each paddlers must have a minimum Class 3 Coast Guard approved PFD available on the water. ACA rules that we earnestly endorse say always wear; don't just have in your possession, a properly fitted and adjusted PFD on the water.
2. A fire extinguisher is not required onboard if your boat doesn't have a motor.
3. A throw-able flotation device is not required if your boat is under 19 feet.
4. Running lights are not required on non-motorized boats under 19 ft. A flashlight IS REQUIRED though, to illuminate your boat after dark. Battery powered green, red, and white lights for starboard, port and stern, respectively are recommended. Common sense says keep an efficient LED headlamp in your emergency gear, just in case, but plan to always be off the water by dark, unless you are planning a night paddle. (Ask around, most experienced paddlers can tell you horror stories about unexpectedly paddling in the dark!)
5. Non-motorized watercraft over 12 feet in length must be licensed on South Dakota waters. Please refer to the section on licensing your boat for more detail.

20 REASONS TO PADDLE A BLACK HILLS LAKE

1. Explore a new area of the Black Hills from a unique vantage point.
2. Paddle with family and friends to share the joy of company and landscape.
3. Have a celebration paddle. Invite a friend or crowd to celebrate a birthday, anniversary, sad, or happy event on the water.
4. Paddle at dawn or sunrise. Every body of water is different in the pre-dawn dark. And the wildlife at that time of day is AMAZING!
5. Paddle through the sunset, or just sit there, rocking in your boat, and take it all in!
6. Paddle solo to be alone and reflect. We say solo with tongue in cheek. Watch the conditions. Always leave a float plan.
7. Paddle at night. Night sounds abound, like bats and nighthawks. The stars, from out on the lake, are unbelievable. You even get an expanded viewing horizon for stars on bigger lakes.
8. Go fishing from your boat where no other type of boat can go!
9. Try fly fishing; a separate world from bait fishing. Attach Velcro to your boat to secure a fly rod and try casting from a canoe/kayak.
10. Paddle as an excellent aerobic exercise.
11. Find a local/regional boat race and get into condition to compete.
12. At a race, drink in the adrenaline rush!
13. Take new folks out and introduce them to your sport.
14. Bird watch, where the birds are not so easily spooked.
15. Observe the animals, which are less threatened by paddle craft.
16. Have a party or barbeque at a handy beach and bring boats. They will be a hit!
17. Have a picnic at a remote shoreline where all have to paddle in.
18. Party out on the lake by rafting up all your friends' boats and make a platform to move about on.
19. Go camping on a remote, previously inaccessible shore of a little Hills lake. You don't have to pack the camp in on your back!
20. Have a lake cleanup where you clean the trash out of otherwise unreachable shores of our beautiful Black Hills lakes and streams!

FIND EM' AND FLOAT EM'

Bob Brown, Legendary National Camp School Aquatics Staff Director, Boy Scouts of America, used this mantra when sending a class of young boaters or prospective aquatic instructors onto the water

Black Hills Lakes to Paddle

Bh lakes.shp
- Angustura Res. Marina
- Angustura Res. North
- Angustura Res. South
- Belle Fourche Res.
- Bismarck Lake Launch
- Canyon Lake Ramp
- Cement Pond Deans Pond
- Center Lk. Beach
- Cold Brook Res. Launch
- Cold BrookRes. out of way
- Cook Lake
- Cottonwood Springs Res
- Cox Lake
- Deerfield Lk. Launch
- Deerfield Lk. N. Remote
- Deerfield Lk. SW Best
- Fort Meade BLM
- Game Lodge Pond
- Hill City Rushmore Jct
- Horsethief Lk pullout
- Horsethief Lk. day use
- Iron Creek Lake
- Lake Alexander BSA
- Lakota Lake
- Legion Lake
- Major Lake
- Mirror Lake East
- Mirror Lake West
- Mitchell Lk. Spillway
- Mitchell Lk. West
- Mud Lake
- Newton Fork Dam
- Pactola Res. Jenny Launch
- Pactola Res. N. Launch
- Pactola Res. S. Beach Launch
- Pactola Res. Visitor Ctr. Trail
- Reusau Lake
- Robaix Lake
- Sheridan Lk. Dakota Pt.
- Sheridan Lk. N. Beach
- Sheridan Lk. South Beach
- Slate Creek Dam
- Stockade Lake Launch
- Stockade Lake West
- Sylvan Lake

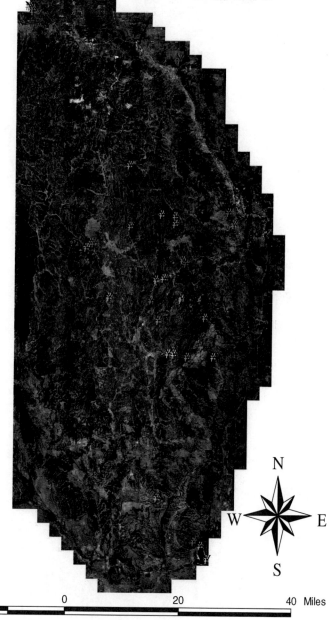

N
W   E
S

20   0   20   40   Miles

7

ABOUT THE NEXT FEW PAGES: TABLE OF INFO ON PADDLING LAKES OF THE BLACK HILLS

Most paddlers coming to the Black Hills are not whitewater boaters. Some of our streams and rivers are appropriate for sea kayaks or recreational (rec) boats; some are a lot more fun in a smaller whitewater boat.

There are lakes in the Black Hills to paddle in boats of any size or type! The following chart illustrates 35 lakes in the Black Hills you can throw a boat in and enjoy the beautiful shore vistas, fish, or just get a workout. While some lakes are used hard by the public, others are hardly used. With this many to choose from, surely you can find more than one lake that helps you answer the old question; "Where will I ever use this boat?"

On the next pages we have compiled a table of 35 Black Hills' paddle-able lakes. Data categories for this table are:

The lake's name(s)

The stream or river that drains the lake

Are motors allowed on the lake? Yes=all boats, Troll= entire lake is a no wake zone, No=no motors allowed

Managing agency and day user fee information.

Size (in surface acres)

GPS waypoint of a good put-in spot in UTM coordinates

Public access yes or no / Directions from a known locale

Following the table, each lake has its own page where long-time paddlers describe some of that lake's highlights and history, hints for the uninitiated, fees and directions to the best put-in/ take-out spots. All lakes are listed alphabetically by common name.

Whatever water you prefer to paddle, please, read the other sections of this guide. A lot of it is applicable to all boaters! Regardless how long you have or have not been paddling, there is always something to learn about staying safe while having fun on the water.

READ ON, WE'LL SEE YOU ON THE WATER!

LAKE NAME	DRAINED BY	MOTORS	MGMT AGENCY USE FEE	SIZE IN ACRES	GPS WAYPOINT (UTM)	ACCESS/ DIRECTIONS
Angostura Reservoir	Cheyenne River	Yes	SDGFP Annual	4275	13T0627987 4798847 13T0629828 4795450	Yes. 2 exits off Hwy 79, south of Hot Springs. Marina, Boat Ramps both exits, many access points
Bear Butte Lake	Belle Fourche River	Yes	SDGFP Annual	125	13T0623715 4924199	Yes. 6 miles northwest of Sturgis off Hwy 79, Opposite base of Bear Butte, Single access road, boat ramp southwest
Bismarck Lake	French Creek	Troll	BHNF Annual	25	13T0619707 4848032	Yes. Just inside Custer State Park, north/opposite Stockade Lake, thru camp loop, Boat Ramp southeast shore
Canyon Lake	Rapid Creek	No	Rapid City No	26	13T0636654 4879879	Yes. West Rapid City, boat ramp west off Chapel Lane Rd, Picnic areas north, spillway
Cement Ponds Dean's Pond	Rapid Creek	No	SDGFP Permit	5	13T0635307 4883076	Yes. Access via SD West River GFP Outdoor Campus. Lake can be used during business hours only.
Center Lake	Battle Creek via Spring Creek	Troll	SDGFP, Annual	25	13T0627061 4851177	Yes. Off Custer State Park Rd 753, via Hwy 16A or Hwy 87. Lake is Behind BH Playhouse. Access thru campground

Lake Name	Drained By	Motors	Mgmt Agency Use Fee	Size in Acres	GPS Waypoint (UTM)	Access/ Directions
Cold Brook Reservoir	Fall River	Troll	Corps of Eng. No	32	13T0622113 4812788	Yes. Access 1 mile west of Hot Springs off of Hwy 385
Cook Lake	Red Water River	Troll	BHNF Annual	27	13T0546907 4938104	Yes. I-90 Exit 199. Wyo Hwy 111 7 miles north. County Rd 144 west to 114 west to Cox Lake sign. 1 mile west to lake
Cottonwood Springs Dam	Fall River	Troll	Corps of Eng. No	25	13T0615687 4810980	Yes. Via driving loop off Hwy 185 miles southwest of Hot Springs
Cox Lake & Mud Lake	Belle Fourche River	No	SDGFP No	3 1	13T0579883 4935106	Yes. I-90 exit at McNenny Nat'l Fish Hatchery. Access 1 mile past hatchery. Cox north of Mud. Mud–no road access
Dalton Lake	Box Elder Creek	No	BHNF Annual	3	13T0621855 4898590	Yes. North of Nemo to Forest Service Rd (FSR) 26 4 miles, east on FSR 224 5 miles. Park at picnic ground southeast shore. Carry boats 50 yds to lake.
Deerfield Lake	Rapid Creek	Troll	BHNF Annual	414	13T0595018 4873916	Yes. West of Hill City on FSR 17, best access is on the south side. Inflow from the south, dam is on the north side.

Lake Name	Drained By	Motors	Mgmt Agency Use Fee	Size in Acres	GPS Waypoint (UTM)	Access/ Directions
Ft Meade Reservoir	Via Belle Fourche R	Troll	BLM No	10	13T0620815 4921597	Yes. 2 miles northeast of Sturgis OR 3 miles southeast of Bear Butte Lake
Game Lodge Pond	Grace Coolidge Creek	No	SDGFP Annual	2	13T0631055 4846602	Yes. Usually restricted to registered campers. East end of meadow at Custer State Park Game Lodge campground.
Grace Coolidge Lakes/ walk-in fishing area	Grace Coolidge Creek	No	SDGFP Annual	7 lakes, each less than 1 acre	13T0627061 4851177 (Center Lake)	Along US Hwy 16A, 1 mile east of Custer State Park headquarters. Or take trailhead off south shore of Center Lake
Horsethief Lake	Spring Creek	Troll	BHNF No	16	13T0621901 4860875	Yes. 5 miles south of Hill City on Hwy 385, 4 miles on Hwy 244. Pull-out on northeast shore, camping on northwest shore, day use area on south shore.
Lake Alexander or Medicine Mountain Lake BSA Lake	Spring Creek	No	Private, No.	10	13T0601644 4861378	Yes. Public use allowed ONLY when scouts are NOT using it. Medicine Mountain Road to Bobcat Road to camp. Talk to the Camp Ranger!

Lake Name	Drained By	Motors	Mgmt Agency Use Fee	Size in Acres	GPS Waypoint (UTM)	Access/ Directions
Lakota Lake	Battle Creek	No	BHNF Annual	11	13T0628702 4856536	Yes. 6 miles south of Keystone on Hwy 16A
Legion Lake	Battle Creek	No	SDGFP Annual	9	13T0623631 4846546	Yes. 5 miles east of Custer on Hwy 16A
Major Lake	Spring Creek	No	Hill City No	4	13T0614775 4865875	Yes. Access via Hill City Football Field
Mirror Lakes	Belle Fourche	No	SDGFP No	9	13T0577283 4934713	Yes. I-90 exit at McNenny National Fish Hatchery, lake access south of hatchery
Mitchell Lake	Spring Creek	No	Hill City No	5	13T0617496 4866275	Yes. 2 miles northeast of Hill City. Next to Hwy 385.
Newton Fork Dam	Spring Creek	No	Hill City No	3	13T0611510 4868845	Yes. 3 miles northwest of Hill City on Deerfield Rd.
Orman Dam or Belle Fourche Reservoir	Belle Fourche	Yes	SDGFP, Annual.	8000	13T0603459 4952353	Yes. Single official access via State Park Rd 8 miles east of Belle Fourche. Rocky Point Rec. Area Boat Ramp. VERY WINDY!

LAKE NAME	DRAINED BY	MOTORS	MGMT AGENCY USE FEE	SIZE IN ACRES	GPS WAYPOINT (UTM)	ACCESS/ DIRECTIONS
Pactola Lake	Rapid Creek	Yes	BHNF Annual	785	13T0616371 4882173 13T0620039 4881959	Yes. Hwy 385 crosses dam. Boat Ramps on both the north and south shore, Marina at south boat ramp. No fee access points at Jenney Gulch & headwaters by Silver City schoolhouse
Reausaw Lake	Box Elder Creek	No	BHNF No	5	13T0610648 4900871	Yes. Nemo Road, 2 miles past Nemo. Not developed, Park on the dam.
Roubaix Lake	Box Elder Creek	No	BHNF Annual	6	13T0607008 4894807	Yes. Exit off Hwy 385, past campground loop to beach.
Sheridan Lake	Spring Creek	Yes	BHNF Annual	385	13T0622196 4870892	Yes. Hwy 385 follows the west shore of the lake. Dam on the northeast. Marina, campground and beach northwest. Picnic, beach southwest; Campground southeast. All are fee areas!
Slate Creek Dam	Rapid Creek	No	BHNF No	3	13T0610212 4877158	Yes. Rochford Rd from Hill City, continue on Mystic Rd, to FSR 249 (gravel.) 8 miles to lake

Lake Name	Drained By	Motors	Mgmt Agency Use Fee	Size in Acres	GPS Waypoint (UTM)	Access/Directions
Stockade Lake	French Creek	Yes	SDGFP Annual	130	13T0619950 4847179	Yes. Hwy 16A 2 miles east of Custer, Multiple access points, access road northwest to west to south sides
Sunday Gulch Pond	Spring Creek	No	BHNF No	2	13T0613458 4860654	Yes. Half mile east of Junction of US Hwy 16/385 and SD Hwy 244.
Sylvan Lake	Spring Creek	No	SDGFP Annual	19	13T0613458 4860654	Yes. Off Hwy 87 in Custer State Park at the base of Harney Peak. Park n' Hike on the southwest shore, Park n' Picnic on the northeast shore.

1 - ANGOSTURA RESERVOIR

Angostura Reservoir was built in 1949 by the United States Bureau of Reclamation as an irrigation project. Since its primary use is irrigation, Angostura's water levels fluctuate wildly. It does however hold a lot of acres of water and is always popular with boaters and campers. Angostura's plentiful natural sand beaches are a big attraction to sun bathers. SDGFP manages the reservoir recreation facilities. There are extensive camping areas, lots of facilities, and three marinas/boat launch areas. All of these facilities are on the eastern and northern sides of the lake. On the west side, paddlers can find semi-secluded shoreline to poke around in with overgrown banks and plentiful shallow snags. For a challenge, put in at the bridge over the Cheyenne River just below Cascade Springs, then float (paddle) into Angostura. Be ready though, you will paddle a lot of shoreline before reaching the northern-most campground roads where you can easily take out.

One cautionary note: Angostura is the closest thing the Black Hills have to open water. Use caution, but know that kayaks are incredibly seaworthy craft. We've had a lot of fun paddling the lake with four foot breaking waves. The Black Hills Paddlers provided safety boater services on Angostura during the 2009 international Primal Quest adventure race in the Black Hills. The wind was so high you couldn't stand up on the exposed shores of the lake and our safety boats and the competitor's kayaks were the only boats on the water for 2 days! Not one

ANGOSTURA RESERVOIR NORTH

person tipped their boat during this event either!

Also, know your boating rules of the road and paddle defensively. Under normal conditions on Angostura, if you paddle anyplace accessible to powerboats, you will be sharing the water with them. Although paddle craft have the right of way, don't assume the approaching motor boater knows the rules of the road for boating. There are also a lot of sailboats on Angostura as it has the most reliable wind west of the Missouri River.

Since Angostura is managed as a South Dakota State Park, You need a State Park Entrance Sticker to access facilities. One of many reasons the $28.00 State Parks annual entrance sticker is such a good deal. It works at every SDGFP managed facility in the state! Without the annual pass a day at Angostura will cost you $6.00/vehicle/day. Camping is not included and will cost $12.00 – $16.00 per night. Showers are included in these fees.

Get to Angostura by driving south of Hot Springs on US Highway 79 for five miles or so. There are two access roads. Both entrances are marked. The first one is for the north side facilities. The second is the much busier and more built up southeast shore. Exit is just two miles further down Highway 79.

ANGOSTURA RESERVOIR SOUTH

2 - BEAR BUTTE LAKE

Think shallow. Think wind! Strictly speaking, this lake is not in the Black Hills. Geologically, however, it is related through proximity to nearby Bear Butte which was uplifted at the same time as the nearby Black Hills, and when it has water enough to out-flow at all, it does eventually drain into the Belle Fourche River which drains a good half of the Black Hills. Bear Butte

Lake also has the distinction of being one of five natural lakes/ponds near the Black Hills and part of its drainage that has no dam. Bear Butte Lake is less than 15 feet deep at its deepest. If it weren't so muddy you could probably walk across half of the lake. Its strong winds can push an unwary boater to the lake's southern shore and make you cry tears of frustration trying to paddle back upwind to the campground or the picnic ground on the lake's western shore (the best put-in/ take-out). Some love the winds. A few hard core Black Hills Paddlers are also avid kite boarders. Watch the sky and you might catch them kite boarding or kite skiing over the lake, depending upon the season.

Bear Butte Lake does not connect directly to Bear Butte State Park, although it is managed as part of the park. Bear Butte Lake and its extended shoreline is a National Wildlife Refuge under the authority of the US Fish and Wildlife Service. As natural wetlands, this helps explain how this shallow, muddy wetlands depression can be a natural lake without a dam when all the lakes in the Hills have dams. Bear Butte State Park and Bear Butte National Wildlife Refuge also share a southern boundary with the BLM managed Fort Meade Recreation Area.

BEAR BUTTE LAKE

Actual management of Bear Butte Lake is handled by SDGFP. So, there is a day use fee which again makes the SD State Parks Annual Pass sticker convenient. Without it your visit to Bear Butte Lake should cost you $6.00/vehicle/day. Camping, of course is extra at 8.00/night. No potable water or showers are available at Bear Butte Lake, by the way. The only facilities are outhouses unless you want to run across the highway to the visitor's center during business hours.

To get to Bear Butte Lake, approach Bear Butte State Park on US Highway

79, 2 miles off of US Highway 34 going northeast from Sturgis. Turn south at the SDGFP sign, west side of the lake.

3 - BISMARCK LAKE

You don't just happen upon Bismarck Lake. It is a BHNF lake, but the only public access is through Custer State Park. Most of the lake is surrounded with steep, rocky banks and it has almost no shore, except at

BECKY & KELLY LANE - BISMARCK LAKE

the dam. For several years, until SDGFP bought its own fleet of rec boats, the Black Hills Paddlers taught kayaking at a workshop on Bismarck Lake. We have great memories of teaching kayaking to SD Outdoors Woman Workshops.

We also did some fabulous night paddling here! Keep a lookout for beaver near the picnic area. Also, watch for turtles. In a cooperative government venture, there is a turtle ramp between Stockade and Bismarck Lakes. This utilizes the existing culvert under highway 16A that divides the two lakes.

Hopefully, you bought an annual user pass/sticker from your local BHNF office, because Bismarck Lake is a National Forest fee area and you will pay $4.00/vehicle/day without the annual sticker. This little gem of a lake has a campground that is heavily used ($19.00/ night, water, flush toilets, no showers). In contrast, an underused picnic area is just past (drive

BISMARCK LAKE

through) the campground with parking, boat launch and shoreline trail over to the dam with several fishing piers. If you take the developed trail, check out the outstanding CCC rockwork on the dam's spillway. The boat ramp is the ONLY public access point on the lake. You might have to share the lake with a very occasional trolling motor, but usually you will be the only watercraft on the lake.

To get to Bismarck Lake, drive into Custer State Park from the Custer side on Highway 16A. One mile into the park, turn left at the Bismarck Lake sign. Drive through the campground to get to the small picnic area for your put-in/take-out.

4 - CANYON LAKE

This is a pretty lake until you look at the water itself. Ick! The water has high levels of nitrates, spikes of coliform counts, and crowds of vegetation, but we Black Hills Paddlers still really like it! Canyon Lake is just minutes from home in Rapid City, and for many of us, our parents grew up swimming in this lake. Also, this is a lake that keeps on trying; trying to clean up its odor, control the "Duck Yuck", hold aquatic vegetation at bay, support some sort of a fishery, establish minimal wetlands in its corners, and to be a positive experience for the thousands who pass by it every day.

Historically, Canyon Lake has a track record of trying as well. Canyon Lake has always been an attraction for Rapid City. While the lake didn't look so "fixed up" years ago, its water quality was actually much better. Canyon Lake has been destroyed by flood twice over the years (1907, 1972). Both times a fatal load of debris piled up against the existing dam face. Flood waters then overflowed the dam top, leading to a total breach. The 1907 flood killed four people, and Canyon Lake Dam was not rebuilt until 1932. After the tragic flood in 1972 which claimed 238 lives, Canyon Lake and its dam were demonized for their contribution to the horrendous loss of life and property. However, Canyon Lake is estimated to have added just 7% to the flood's total crest that horrible night. While definitely a factor in the downstream loss of life and property destruction the dam's failure was not a major contributor. Today's Canyon Lake intentionally bears little resemblance to its predecessor. The dam is now sloped, designed to have water safely flow over the top. Banks are designed to remain stable and resist erosion. With the island in the middle and its jutting causeway, circulation patterns have been modified. Finally, there is simply less water impounded now in the relatively shallow lake.

Today, water quality is improved, as the large flock of over-wintering birds is gone and Rapid City is enforcing a no-feed ordinance for waterfowl.

Black Hills Paddlers can once again recommend Canyon Lake as a nice paddle (with some reservation)! There is still a large amount of "Duck Yuck" entombed in the sediment, and water-weed proliferates on the dam side of the island, which is an entanglement hazard for swimmers.

HALLOWEEN PADDLE ON CANYON LAKE

Canyon Lake is on the west end of Rapid City, along US Highway 44. The best place to put in/ take-out is at the west side parking area and boat ramp. The lake is managed as part of the extensive Rapid City Parks System. No fees, no services, no motors, either. You might venture upstream a few yards and get a feel for the in-flowing current. Perhaps you even want to put on a skirt and helmet and join some of us in running the spillway. Just the first dam, please. Dams 2 and 3 are low head boat beaters that recirculate at high flows! All in all, though a nice little lake that keeps on trying, just don't drink the water; yet!

5 - CEMENT PLANT POND/ DEAN'S POND

Paddling this small pond puts you under the watchful eye of the brand new (as of Oct, 2011) West River headquarters, and Outdoor Campus for the SDGFP. The Outdoor Campus has its own fleet of kayaks and canoes and offers classes for local folks in all manner of outdoor aquatic pursuits on the pond. The name of this pond can create a local argument. When casually called Cement Plant Pond, local folks, including several Black Hills Paddlers who grew up near here take exception to that name. They point out, quite correctly, that Cement Plant Pond is down *there*, the quarry pond by the cement plant. This pond is actually one of four ponds on the now state-owned property. The largest of the four ponds, and the pond that the new West River Outdoor Campus faces, is correctly named Dean's Pond. It is named after the family who historically owned Dean's Pond before the land was acquired by Hills Materials Company, who in turn sold/donated it to the state of South Dakota.

To get to SDGFP's Outdoor Campus West, drive west on Main Street/Sturgis Road to the west edge of Rapid City. Turn south on Adventure Drive just west of the bowling alley. The most convenient put-in/ take-out is on the sand/gravel beach south of the parking lot. For Outdoor Campus security, please visit/paddle during business hours only. Please also call the Outdoor Campus at 605-394-6072 before you drop by in case the water is occupied with an event or class. No official services, but the Outdoor Campus West building is impressive, and they do have bathrooms inside. Stop in and browse the Outdoor Campus West facility. Be sure and check out the nature trails.

6 - CENTER LAKE

Center Lake was built in the 1930's by the CCC amidst a flurry of other public works across the nation. You can paddle right up to the edge of the dam and in just seconds have a wild vista before you; driving home the idea that dams make a beautiful vantage point. The lake is long enough that from the dam the campground is out of site. Local Boy Scouts grew up camping at this lake every November as a cautionary deference to hunting season in the surrounding BHNF. In those long ago days, Scouts would camp in what is now the day use facility surrounding the southwest shore beach.

Day-use facilities have been expanded on both shores of the lake, and all camping is now sprawled along both sides of the lake access road, just upstream of the lake. Like Bismarck Lake, you can't just happen onto Center Lake. You must drive through the campground to reach it. The "newer" day use facilities are around the lake on the north shore, including a boat ramp. This would be your official put-in/ take-out spot. There is also a very nice sandy beach on the southwest shore of the lake that is even handier to launch a boat next to.

WARNING **Do not launch or land your boat on a marked swim beach. You will be ticketed!**

Trolling motors are allowed at Center Lake, but the rare motorboat is almost always a dedicated fisher, and likely to ignore you even more effectively than you ignore them.

Hopefully, you have purchased the $28.00 SD State Parks annual access pass. Otherwise you will be charged $14.00/vehicle for a 7 day pass. Everybody say together, "ANNUAL PASS, YES!" Camping at Center Lake is called semi-modern. This means vault toilets, but also fresh water and access to a central shower facility, all for $18.00 per night.

You very intentionally get to Center Lake off of SD Highway 753, via US Hwy 16A or SD Hwy 87. Center Lake is behind the Black Hills Playhouse. Access Center Lake through the campground entrance partway up the hill west of the Playhouse.

7 - COLD BROOK RESERVOIR

Cold Brook could almost be considered Hot Springs' private swimming hole. Any time school is out and the sun warms the water a bit, this lake just seems to sprout kids. Grab your boat and join them! Cold Brook and Cottonwood Springs are both flood control facilities built and operated by the US Army Corps of Engineers on the *dry* side of the Black Hills just upstream of Hot Springs, SD. The resulting structures are massive! At first we thought that flood control facilities of this magnitude were some sort of a joke, being built on these usually very dry south-facing slopes of the Black Hills. History does teach those who listen, though and a look back shows quite a history of massive run-off water flooding this very popular resort community. Thanks to the National Weather Service Weather Forecast Office, for these stats.

"The design document for Cottonwood Springs Dam indicates a report from "pioneer residents" of a peak stage in 1884 that was 6 feet higher than the 1938 flood. The design document for Cold Brook Dam indicates historical high-water marks for the same 1883 date that are 7 feet higher than in 1937, with the 1937 flow shown as about 15 percent larger than the 1938 flow. 1937 flooding caused an estimated $200,000 in damage in Hot Springs. In 1938 a discharge of 13,100 CFS was recorded at the Hot Spring river gauge. Then, in 1947 there was once again flooding along Fall River (prior to completion of Cold Brook Reservoir)."

Both reservoirs are direct outcomes of the 1941 Federal Flood Control Act.

No day use fees are charged here and camping is just $7.00/night at either "reservoir." Oddly, more heavily used Cold brook has only vault toilets while out-of-the-way Cottonwood Springs has flush toilets. No showers are available at either lake. Finally; water, no matter how tame the lake or

COLD BROOK RESERVOIR

stream seems, is ever entirely safe. In July, 2009 a solo boater from Hot Springs died on Cold Brook Reservoir, likely when his red Otter rec boat capsized in a sudden thunderstorm and the paddler drowned. In an unsettling twist, the kayak was never found. It would seem someone found the boat drifted against shore and took it? Please, follow recommended safety guidelines. Paddle safe!

The turnoff to Cold Brook is just a mile West of Hot Springs on highway 385. 2 blocks and the road will take you to the right and up into a canyon. Follow the road up over the BIG dam and around the lake. There is a pretty little campground right at the head of the lake. Day use areas are further down the road on the south shore. There is a steep gravel ramp next to a very tall dock for you to put-in/take-out. Or, drive a few more yards to the end of the road. This is just out of sight of the busy sand beach and you can easily carry your boat to the water. **Do not launch or land your boat on a marked swim beach. You will be ticketed!**

8 - COOK LAKE

Cook Lake is the only paddle-able lake in the Black Hills of Wyoming. Some might argue that Cook Lake is in the Bear Lodge Mountains and not part of the Black Hills. However, Cook Lake is managed as a separate district in an ecologically connected Black Hills National Forest. Geologically and ecologically, the Black Hills and the Bear Lodge Mountains are *joined at the hip*, so to speak. From a paddler's viewpoint, these two prairie forests are also connected. Cook Lake and the Bear Lodge Mountains drain via the Red Water River into the Belle Fourche River and ultimately the Cheyenne River which drains all of the Black Hills.

The Bear Lodge Mountains that host Cook Lake have some serious history. The area was settled in the 1880's by prospectors and eventually ranchers who

COOK LAKE

prospected and drove cattle down the waterways following mountain streams to access the rugged Bear Lodge Mountain slopes. Cook Lake dams one of those streams that served as an early road for prospectors and ranchers. Today, an established trail system in these rugged canyons is home to the highly ranked Fat Tire Mountain Bike Race.

Cook Lake charges a $3.00 day use fee, or $15.00 for an annual pass. The lake has beautiful picnic areas spread around two sides served by the access road. Campground is at the south end of the lake. Camping is $9.00/night. No showers, vault toilets, drinking water is available seasonally.

Getting to Cook Lake can be a challenge. It is almost a two hour drive from Rapid City. The Black Hills Paddlers didn't have any good photographs of Cook Lake for this article, and by the time we got out to remedy that omission, snow had already covered the lake, leaving us to make a combination photo shoot, scouting run to Cook Lake with 4-wheel drive and tire chains. In better weather conditions accessing Cook Lake is pretty straight-forward, just 15 miles north of Sundance, Wyoming. Since the road from Sundance is less passable in winter, we took the *shortcut* from Rapid City, taking the second Wyoming exit off I-90, exit 199, then north on Wyoming Highway 111 for 7 miles. Turn left on County Road 144, continuing west as the road turns into County Road 114. Turn right at the Cook Lake sign. It is one mile down the hill to Cook Lake. After getting some photos of the by then frozen and snow covered Cook Lake, we nearly had to chain up the 4WD pickup truck to get back up the first mile of hill!

9 - COTTONWOOD SPRINGS RESERVOIR

At first glance, Cottonwood Springs and Cold Brook reservoirs look like virtual twins. Look just a bit closer and differences abound, although both are owned

COTTONWOOD SPRINGS RESERVOIR

and managed by the US Army Corps of Engineers and are designed to be effective at flood control. Cold Brook is heavily used while Cottonwood Springs is much more lightly used.

This recreation area is terribly under-used: Yeah! No day use fees, either. Services include boat launch, flush toilets, potable water. Camping is just $7.00/night. Don't expect a crowd, but don't expect a lot of water, either. The lake can shrink up to nearly nothing in dry years. Enjoy a solitary paddle on this remarkably isolated lake. Stare up at the seemingly massively overbuilt dam. Then reflect on how quickly our Black Hills streams have turned deadly as they flush surface water out of the Hills and into the underground aquifers.

You get to Cottonwood Springs Dam by driving 5 miles west of Hot Springs on US Highway 18. Take the marked turnoff. A gravel road winds back north. Eventually you crest a hill which you will discover is actually a massive flood control dam. Below you spread the recreation facilities. The campground loop on your right is fairly high above the south shore of the lake. Follow the access road around the head of the lake to the day use facilities and boat launch (put-in/take out here) on the north shore.

10 & 11 - COX LAKE & MUD LAKE

We treat these two lakes together because they are right next to each other with a single access point. While neither lake is in the Black Hills proper, they are perched at the edge of the highly erodible outer rim of the Black Hills. Both drain into the Red Water River, which then drains into the Belle Fourche River. Cox and Mud Lakes are two of the five lakes outside the Black Hills proper that do not have a dam.

According to the South Dakota Place Names Dictionary. there are 15 Mud Lakes in South Dakota,

COX LAKE

including another in the Black Hills. The Mud Lake by Cox Lake is by far the largest and the only one in or near the Black Hills that is paddle-able. The other Mud Lake in the Black Hills is in the Castle Creek headwaters between Rochford and Black Fox. It is just a marshy wide spot in the meadow. Not enough open water to even float a boat!

No fees, no services, no campground, just a small fishing dock and a lonely vault toilet at the end of the road accessing Cox Lake. The driveway to the fishing dock is the only access to put your boat in on either lake. These lakes are not remote, but they are virtually unknown. Take the opportunity to discover and paddle these surprising, right

MUD LAKE

under our noses prairie sinkhole lakes in the sedimentary outer rim of the Black Hills.

To get to Cox and Mud Lakes, travel I-90 west of Spearfish almost to the Wyoming line. The last exit in South Dakota is to the McNenny Fish Hatchery. Follow the signs to McNenny, then continue past the fish hatchery about half-mile until the road shortly takes a big jog. Stay left on McNenny Road after the jog, and you will see both lakes to your right. There is an access road just ¼ mile down the McNenny Road from the big jog that winds down to the fishing dock on Coxes Lake.

12 - DALTON LAKE

Dalton Lake is another of those places you have to *want* to go to get there. When Black Hills Paddlers last visited Dalton Lake, the lake, campground and day use area was closed for reconstruction and the lake had been drained. The USFS contractor was doing some major drainage revisions and refilled the lake in the spring of 2012. The age of Dalton Lake is unknown. It feeds Elk Creek which has seen some big flooding over the years.

BHNF Recreation day user fees apply at Dalton Lake , so it is $4.00/day to park and paddle unless you've got your BHNF Annual Recreation User Pass on your windshield. Camping is $15.00/night. A single hand-pump gives potable water and there are vault toilets to use. No Showers. There is a nice sidewalk on the south shore with fishing piers. The easiest boat access is from the south shore sidewalk.

DALTON LAKE

To get to Dalton Lake, go to Nemo. Stay on the Nemo Road two miles past (northwest of) Nemo. Turn right (north) on the Vanocker Canyon Road. Four miles down this road there will be a USFS sign directing you right (East). Four miles to the end of this road is Dalton Lake. Day user parking is at the Centennial Trail Trailhead just past the campground.

13 - DEERFIELD LAKE

This is a sparkling mountain lake with a twinkle in its eye. Or at least, if a lake could *twinkle*, this lake would! Number three of the four biggest Lakes in the Black Hills, Deerfield is the classic middle child. It feels no pressure to be more than it is, and goes about doing that with a knowing grin in its waves. The waters of Deerfield Lake, like the other large lakes in the Black Hills, Pactola, Sheridan and Stockade, each literally cover a bit of History. In the case of Deerfield Lake, a major campsite of General George A Custer's 1874 expedition to the Black Hills sits on ground now inundated by Deerfield's waters.

DEERFIELD RESERVOIR

Comfortably ensconced in its *middle child* position, Deerfield is tasked with some flood protection, but not too much due to the relatively close Pactola Reservoir downstream. The water of Deerfield Reservoir is intended to benefit downstream users, but that user base is changing as fewer downstream irrigators now call for water from bigger Pactola Reservoir, much less smaller Deerfield. Deerfield serves a fairly busy role as a recreation source, but more to the less populated northern Hills, since Rapid City users are closer to the bigger Pactola and Sheridan Lakes. All-in-all, Deerfield reservoir serves many functions, yet none of them seem to stress the reservoir too much. You will enjoy a nice, long paddle on this *middle child* lake that remains a very nice place to "do your thing!"

For day use, your Annual BHNF Recreation Pass is handy. Otherwise the day user's recreation fee is 4.00 per vehicle per day. BTW: Power boats are welcome on Deerfield, but are usually quite benign to paddlers because the whole lake is a no-wake zone. All campgrounds have potable water, vault toilets and no showers. Camping here costs $15.00 per night.

Get to Deerfield Reservoir by taking the Deerfield road out of Hill City and follow the signs. Three spots are good put-ins. The boat launch for power boats is at the end of the road past Dutchman loop which is the first Deerfield lake drive you come to from Hill City. The Whitetail campground and loop is further west off of the Deerfield road. For the *best* put-in go to the west end of Whitetail Loop then back down the loop road to a picnic ground right next to the lake. There is an old dirt ramp down to the lake. The third good put-in is all the way around

PICNIC GROUND - DEERFIELD RESERVOIR

on the north shore of the lake. Stay on the Rochford Road as it hooks around the lake to the north. Turn on County Road 417 (looks like a pasture entrance) and bounce down this unimproved road to the Custer Trail Campground, boat launch, picnic area.

14 - FT MEADE RESERVOIR, FT MEADE BLM

Some years this small lake is just a mud puddle. However, when it has water, which it does in wet years or in the spring, it is a paddle to rival the views of Bear Butte Lake without the wind. No camping, no services, no fees; just a small parking lot with a vault toilet. Easy access to the water.

The small lake can be a challenge to find from nearby Sturgis because you must cross the town and climb the switchback out of Woodle Field in the creek bottom. It is easier to turn off SD Highway 79 at the west side of Bear Butte Lake and stay on the gravel road as it swings east. Lake access road is north off the gravel road at the southern edge of the "reservoir."

15 - GAME LODGE POND

Built in 1920, the Custer State Park Game Lodge was a summer vacation spot for President Calvin Coolidge in 1927. Three generations of locals still refer to it as the "summer white house." At the east edge of the big campground meadow that the Game Lodge looks out over is this little lake/pond.

GAME LODGE POND

If you have your Custer State Park entrance pass, go ahead and pull off onto the wide shoulder of Highway 16A and drop your boat in. Fed by tiny Grace Coolidge Creek, most of the use this pond sees is as a swimming hole for the Game Lodge Campground in the big meadow upstream.

16 - GRACE COOLIDGE WALK-IN FISHING AREA

When you look at tiny Grace Coolidge Pond along the highway, you have to think, "Why bother?" The pond is barely the size of a swimming pool. We include this pond in the guide, though, not to insult paddlers, but to open a question. Did you know there seven more small ponds above this first Grace Coolidge Pond? To the best of our knowledge these ponds, dating back to when the CCC built upstream Center Lake, have NEVER been paddled. Collectively, this is the Grace Coolidge Walk-in Fishing Area. There is a walking trail From Grace Coolidge Lake three miles up to Center Lake. The trail follows Grace Coolidge Creek, passing close to each of the little ponds. Each pond is close to an acre in size. To remind hikers that they are following a creek, the trail crosses Grace Coolidge Creek 15 times! Paddling these lakes would take some planning and likely a packable, inflatable boat. Drop a boat in Grace Coolidge Pond sometime to check it out. The Pond is on the North side of US Highway 16A, just a mile west of the Park Headquarters. No services! Be sure you have your SD State Parks Annual entrance sticker before you park and hike, or park and paddle! Otherwise, cost is $14.00/vehicle/week.

17 - HORSETHIEF LAKE

Most visitors to the Black Hills have no idea what they are passing as they zoom by this lake on the back side of Mt Rushmore. Horsethief Lake campground is one of the most popular, and busy camping destinations in the Black Hills. Horsethief Lake has recently added really nice day use facilities as well and the lake sees minimal boat traffic. The headwaters of the lake look just like you would imagine a mountain lake inflow choked with down timber should. Happy exploring!

HORSETHIEF LAKE DAY USE AREA

Horsethief Lake, built in 1940, drains into Battle Creek and on to the Cheyenne River. Most of the smaller lakes high in the Hills have little to do with downstream flooding impact. These lakes just don't impound enough water, nor do they normally have much downstream development to be considered a hazard. However, in a recent flood hazard survey of small mountain lakes in the Black Hills, Horsethief Lake Dam was rated as a significant dam break hazard because of significant development and a large campground just a short distance downstream

Camping costs $21.00 per day and gives you access to potable water, a vault toilet and no showers. We typically just day paddle Horsethief as camp sites are hard to come by. Recreation managers say this is probably the most heavily used campground in the Black Hills National Forest. Even with the quality of this lake and its nice day use facilities, USFS does not charge day users a recreation fee at Horsethief. I guess that is just another reason this lake is a favorite!

Horsethief Lake is tucked behind Mt Rushmore. Access from Mt Rushmore is via SD Highway 244 or go six miles up SD Highway 244 from the junction of SD Highway 244/US Highway 385 three miles south of Hill City. Coming from Hill City the first Horsethief Lake access you come to is the turn to Horsethief Lake Campground. Access to the lake from the campground is limited to registered campers. The second Horsethief Lake access point is the dam itself. There is a pull-off on top of the dam where we used to have to put-in/take out our boats. It was a rocky scramble! Fortunately, just a half mile further south brings you to the newer access for hikers and day users. The forest service has constructed a very nice day use/trailhead facility here. It has vault toilets, a great parking area and a shoreline trail with fishing piers. This also gives very easy access to launch or load boats. No potable water is accessible to day users.

18 - IRON CREEK LAKE

Wow! Talk about pristine! Iron Creek Lake is just remote enough to avoid most traffic. It is a hoot to scramble around on the dam. The 1936 Works Progress Administration (WPA) brass plaque is still sitting right in the open near the dam. Apparently built for fishing and recreation, Black Hills Paddlers thinks nobody told the public, because this lake is just like it was

75 years ago! In recent years a fairly good-sized XTerra triathlon race has been based at Iron Creek Lake. Black Hills Paddlers provides safety boaters for the swim part of this race. Events like this are building a very appreciative user-base for a new generation of lake users.

There are no day user fees. Camping is $14.00 per night with access to flush toilets and showers for campers. Vault toilet and camp store available for day users seasonally. Drop a boat in and knock around this gem of a lake. There is even a hidden waterfall.

IRON CREEK LAKE

To get to iron Creek Lake, take the Tinton Road out of Spearfish for 13 miles. At a handmade wooden sign, turn west on Beaver Creek Road. After ½ mile, another wooden sign directs you south to Iron Creek Lake. There is a summer cabin group at the south end of the lake and a picnic ground on the west shore. A private store and campground surround the sandy public beach. There is even a dock/boat ramp next to the beach which is the logical put-in/take out.

19 - LAKE ALEXANDER

Black Hills Paddler Kelly spent four wonderful summers teaching boating on this lake. It is fun to poke about in the wetlands that seem to choke the head of the lake. However, the lake is still young (1974) and quite healthy. It can be a bit tough to access Lake Alexander because the lake was built on historic Medicine Mountain Ranch which is now an award-winning Boy Scout Camp. In exchange for stocking the Lake, SDGFP and BSA have an agreement that the lake is public access whenever Scouts are not in camp. However, the Boy Scouts use their camp most weekends and nearly all summer. It's a great paddle for a weekday, though. Call the camp ranger (605-673-2790) so he is expecting you. There are no public services here at all. FYI: Also called Boy Scout Lake or Medicine Mountain Lake, Lake Alexander is officially named in memory of a promising, local, young-adult Scouter whose life ended far too early.

Medicine Mountain Scout Ranch is located in the Custer Limestone country, along Bobcat Road, which connects with Limestone Road off of Highway 16/385 above Custer at the Fort. Follow the brown and white Forest Service signs. WITH the Camp Ranger's permission, access the lake by driving south through the camp following the creek to the lake. Drive up the dam face and you will see a nice sand beach to put-in/take-out on. Drive carefully.

20 - LAKOTA LAKE

Biltmore Lake was built by a private party in 1963. The lake was purchased by the USFS around 1969 and renamed Lakota Lake. The lake drains a larger section of the Hills than other small lakes high in the Black Hills. However, it is considered a low dam break hazard because of sparse development downstream. Recreation is the lake's listed use, so use it!

Lakota Lake is a nice paddle. It is big enough to get a workout, small enough that you see the whole lake from the shore. There has been some significant siltation in the lake over its young life (estimated at 25% in 1998) which has formed some nice cattail patches to go exploring in.

LAKOTA LAKE

There is no camping at Lakota Lake, but it has a nice picnic area on the northwest shore with great access to the water for your boat. There is no potable water but there is one vault toilet available to use.

35

Recreation users need an annual Recreation Pass on your windshield or will have to pay $4.00 per vehicle per day to park-n-paddle at Lakota Lake.

Lakota Lake is conveniently located just off the north side of US Highway 16A, midway between the Iron Mountain Lookout and the Playhouse road junction.

21 - LEGION LAKE

Legion Lake is busy all summer! The lodge is built right against the lake, and it feels like you are walking across someone's back yard to put your boat in. When the sun is shining and the water is warming up, this lake does a good traffic in boat rentals, swimmers and fishing, but it is not a big lake, and when all the rental boats are on the water it can feel more like you are paddling in a pool rather than a mountain lake. There is a short hiking trail all the way around Legion Lake, but the headwaters of the Lake are pretty marshy which does give paddlers some feeling of privacy to pole around in.

LEGION LAKE

Legion Lake and Lodge have a history older than Custer State Park itself. In 1897, when South Dakota was just eight years old, the United States

Congress gave the State of South Dakota sections 16 and 36 of every township in the state to use as school lands. Administering these widely spread sections of isolated timber in the Black Hills was virtually impossible so, in 1910, after 4 years of negotiations, South Dakota gave up the school land sections in the Black Hills Forest Reserve in exchange for what became Custer State Forest in 1912. Custer State Park began as a game preserve in the Custer State Forest. At that time the Legion Lake area was leased by the local American Legion post, thus the resort and lake's current name. Custer State Park grew rapidly in the 1920's. Legion Lake itself was a CCC project in the 1930's as our nation worked to dig itself out of recession.

The best put-in/take-out is the grass, west side of the rental dock. Parking can be very crowded in the summer. There are good services available: nice restrooms, a restaurant and store, boat rentals and a swimming beach. **Do not launch or land your boat on a marked swim beach. You will be ticketed!** There is no campground right at the lake, camping cabins only on the lake side. The campground with flush toilets and showers is north just across the highway. Cost for camping is $20.00/night. You don't need an entrance pass to travel by Legion lake on the state highway, but you do if you plan to stop and look around or paddle. Bring your $28.00 annual pass for all SD State Parks or pay $14.00 for a one week pass.

You can get to Legion Lake most directly from Custer. Enter Custer State Park East of Custer on highway 16A. 7 miles to Legion Lake.

22 - MAJOR LAKE

"Major" is a huge exaggeration for this pond. It is neither big nor deep. The only thing major about it is the name. However, it is a nice little paddle, and very convenient. We admit, this is more a paddle to say you've done it rather than for any loftier goal. There are no fees, no camping, no service to speak of, just a lone porta-potty if you got to go. Even though no services here, you are in the middle of Hill City, a delightful little town with great food and shopping just down the street!

Major Lake sits in the middle of Hill City, right next to the Mickelson Trail. The access road is 1 block east of the Hill City post office. This is also access for the Hill City football field and track. The only place to put-

GEESE ON MAJOR LAKE

in/take-out is along the mowed north shore. Go, Hill City Rangers!

23 - MIRROR LAKES

Upper and lower Mirror Lakes are hands down the most beautiful water in and around the Black Hills. The physical setting for Mirror Lakes is not ostensibly beautiful, but it is striking by prairie standards. These are two of the five natural lakes on the prairie closely surrounding the Black Hills. Both Mirror Lakes are sink-holes in the very water-soluble gypsum layer surrounding the outer rim of the Black Hills. The depth of these sinkholes and their capacity to hold water, instead of flushing themselves into a subterranean toilet bowl, is unknown. When paddling here be sure to let the lake water settle, and then peer into the clear mineralized green depths of the lake.

Both Mirror Lakes have close, accessible driveways and parking. Each lake has several fishing piers that jut out into the water. The best put-in/take-out is near the fishing piers as they are placed on the most accessible shores. These are small lakes that lend to a short paddle but are still captivating waters! Enjoy! There no fees, no camping, no services except a vault toilet, no potable water available, and no picnic tables. Just sublimely beautiful water!

You get to Mirror Lakes by exiting I-90 west of Spearfish at the last South

Dakota exit (McNenny). Follow signs to the McNenny Fish Hatchery. Just before turning into McNenny is the sign to Mirror Lakes, which are almost directly behind the fish hatchery. Mirror Lakes are often confused with the nearby, less visited Cox and Mud Lakes which are another mile past McNenny Fish Hatchery.

24 - MITCHELL LAKE

To really get a lesson on siltation (the buildup of sediment) and eutrophication (the overgrowth of vegetation caused by excess nutrients, usually from runoff), drop your boat into Mitchell Lake. Odds are pretty good that you've driven by this lake many, many times and never even realized there was a real lake in all that silt and cattail.

MITCHELL LAKE

Mitchell Lake was built in 1936. Its listed purpose is day use, fishing, and some stream flow control. This little lake was never very big, deep or significant in flood control because Sheridan Lake is just 4 miles downstream.

MITCHELL LAKE -SPILLWAY

The lake is now pretty well choked off at its headwaters, which you look at for a long time when driving from the Three Forks junction of Highways 16 and 385 into Hill City. Turn at the small green/white Mitchell Lake road sign to look at the dam. The lake looks nice from here and there is parking but no good place to launch a boat. The best put in/takeout is west of here along the highway. You can find several spots where firm ground goes to the water. You will have to park on the shoulder but it is quite wide here as a number of fly fishers frequent this lake and park there. No fees, no services, no development of any sort just a nice little mountain lake that is a living laboratory example of eutrophication in a riparian meadow.

25 - NEWTON FORK DAM

We listed this dam, as with several others, to give paddlers some new lakes to paddle, "just to say you did!" Located just three miles northwest of Hill City on the Deerfield Road, Newton Fork Dam is handy, if small. The dam is on the south side of the road. Take the access driveway to park.

NEWTON FORK DAM

Put in anywhere on the west shore. No fees, no potable water, no services except a vault toilet.

26 - ORMAN DAM

The Belle Fourche Irrigation Project is the Bureau of Reclamation's name for this ambitious irrigation project to water crops on the surrounding prairie. This makes for some wildly fluctuating water levels. The dam was built from 1907-1911, making Orman one of the area's oldest impoundments. At the time of its construction Orman Dam was the largest earthen dam in the world! Technically, this lake is well outside the Black Hills. However, after spring run-off from snowmelt and rain, irrigation demand is the biggest factor in how much water the Belle Fourche River delivers to the Cheyenne and Missouri Rivers. Since some of Black Hills Paddlers' favorite paddles are on the Cheyenne and Belle Fourche Rivers, Orman Dam becomes important to paddlers, even if not technically in the Black Hills.

Few of us actually paddle Orman Dam regularly due to weather and distance. Black Hills Paddlers members who live in the Northern Hills and Belle Fourche do get on the reservoir more frequently and find it a challenging, but rewarding paddle. Our kite boarding members love it too, because it is WINDY! It is easy to start out in the early morning calm, get downwind of your take-out, and have the wind come up with a vengeance! Trying to paddle a mile or two against the wind with your body acting like a human sail while whitecaps are breaking over the gunwales of your boat is NOT FUN! OR SAFE! In recent years a high wind alarm was installed at the Rocky Point recreation area. When the alarm siren sounds, get off the water! Good sized motorboats have swamped in the rush to get them out of the water at the Rocky Point boat ramp during high winds. Orman Dam's shoreline and wildlife is spectacular when calm, and most of the prettier areas are upwind of the prevailing westerly's, but be prepared!

SDGFP manages the Belle Fourche Reservoir Recreation Area for the Bureau of Reclamation. Most of the reservoir area is also part of the Belle Fourche National Wildlife Refuge, so recreation development is concentrated in one area called Rocky Point. Rocky Point looks like a finger pointing into the middle of the lake. There are lots of facilities here! Better bring your South Dakota State Parks Annual Entrance sticker, because without it, day users pay $4.00/vehicle/day. Camping and picnic facilities are both available at Rocky Point. Facilities include some flush toilets, a shower house, potable water, a playground, paddle craft rentals, a boat launch (the best place to put-in/ take-out), even a fish cleaning station!

To get to Belle Fourche Reservoir (Orman Dam) and Rocky Point Recreation Area take US Highway 212 east out of Belle Fourche City for eight miles. Turn north at the sign to Rocky Point. Before you come to the Rocky Point Recreation Area, you will cross the Belle Fourche Irrigation Project inlet canal that comes from a very dangerous diversion dam six miles upstream on the Belle Fourche River. There is almost NO natural inflow to this reservoir. So when irrigators call for water LOTS of it can come gushing down this inlet canal from where it is diverted from the Belle Fourche River. Stay out of this diversion dam! Following is an explanation of just how dangerous this inflow can be.

27- BELLE FOURCHE RIVER DIVERSION DAM

The Belle Fourche diversion dam is a deadly hazard on the Belle Fourche River and it is also called a dam, which could mislead paddlers not familiar with the area. **This is no place for paddlers!** The diversion dam is not a dam in the sense of a water impoundment. It is the junction where the Bureau of Reclamation diverts water from the Belle Fourche River through a 6 ½ mile long upstream diversion ditch to feed the Belle Fourche Reservoir, also known as Orman Dam. The upstream diversion dam diverts water from the Belle Fourche River into Crow Creek Valley where it forms the Belle Fourche River water storage reservoir for the Bureau of Reclamation's very ambitious Belle Fourche Irrigation project.

BELLE FOURCHE DIVERSION BASIN

DIVERSION DAM GATE HYDRAULICS

This diversion dam is **DEADLY TO PADDLERS**. On older maps it is listed as a dam because at one point in time there was an impoundment of water at the diversion site. Unfortunately, that impoundment area is now silted in and paddlers are funneled into a death trap straight through the BIG gates of the diversion project. This gate has no safe eddy lines, multiple, deadly, recirculating hydraulics, all with no safe egress. Once you come around the blind corner, your boat will be pushed through this gate and there is no safe line to run through the gate even for an expert boater. This is a Class VI man-made rapid. Please do not even consider running this, it is dangerous, and now illegal!

These hydraulics are the unfortunate site of a triple fatality in the summer of 2010. The diversion dam section of The Belle Fourche River is now **CLOSED TO RIVER USERS!**

Coming from upstream we recommend a very nice take-out at City

BELLE FOURCHE RIVER CLOSURE SIGN

Park in the center of Belle Fourche City. Start looking for a boater-friendly gap in the deeply cut river bank as soon as you see the big flag at the Belle Fourche Visitor Center/ Center of the Nation monument. If you don't take out here your take-out further downstream will be ugly, muddy, miserable, and possibly deadly! The actual river closure area is at the FIRST bridge across the Belle Fourche River just east of the town of Belle Fourche. Next easiest place to put-in again is where the Belle Fourche River crosses Highway 212 a second time, 6 miles DOWNSTREAM (east) of the reservoir. **Stay out of this death trap, please!**

28 - PACTOLA RESERVOIR

The Black Hills Paddlers feel like Pactola is our home lake. Pactola's charms have encouraged us to sponsor several annual paddle events based out of the Silver City Community Hall at the head of Pactola. Jenney Gulch is our primary venue to teach introductory boating. Chad Andrew's

JENNY GULCH

Intro to whitewater classes (ACA certified) uses Rapid Creek as it flows into Pactola. Another of Pactola's many charms is all the acres of wetlands at the head of the lake. Paddle from Jenney Gulch up to the schoolhouse or do the reverse and paddle downstream. Pactola is a pretty heavily used recreation area, yet from Jenney Gulch upstream is a no-wake zone. Below the well camouflaged parking area across from the Silver City Community Hall you will almost always find wonderful wildlife, no other boats and just a bit of creek current at the top. Black Hills Paddlers Paulette and Nancy have hung out in these headwaters so much that they are on a first name basis with the resident beavers, eagles and osprey!

Pactola by the dam is also very special in the late fall when ice is forming. It is huge fun to jump the boats on and off the ice. Dress for it please! Bring ice tools and a rope. Black Hills Paddlers hosts an annual New Year's Eve event focused around this fun. Hint: Boats skate the best in reverse! This is an activity where rec boats rule!

Pactola Lake is the largest of the four big lakes *in* the Black Hills proper. Like the other three, Sheridan, Deerfield and Stockade Lakes, Pactola inundates a lot of history. The town of Pactola under Lake Pactola was named by drunken miners after the ancient Greek's placer diggings on the mythical river Pactolus. Before the miners renamed their town Pactola, it was known as Camp Crook. General Crook made his headquarters in the valley in 1876 while he tried to chase miners out of the hills for violating the US treaty with the Lakota. During these early years Pactola boasted the first post office in Pennington County and bemoaned the lawless element that also frequented the valley.

YOGA FUN AT PACTOLA RESERVOIR

Construction began on the 240 foot-tall Pactola Dam in 1952 and finished in 1956. The result was a lake that caused buildings to either be moved or abandoned in the entire valley. These including a CCC camp, several church camps and individual dwellings all the way upstream to present day Silver City.

As the largest reservoir *in* the Black Hills, primary uses of Pactola water include: supplying water to downstream users, flood control, and of lesser importance, recreation. Subsequently the water levels in Pactola Lake fluctuate a lot! These fluctuations are hard on commercial development but we paddlers love it for the late season flows it can bring to Rapid Creek.

Pactola's popularity with transient power boats has made it a magnet for exotic species of flora and fauna. Pactola is almost the only West River site

for several different invasive species. (See SD Boat Wash Program pages for specifics.) However, Pactola Lake might provide the key to controlling a particularly

EVENING PADDLE ON PACTOLA – JUSTIN HERREMAN

obnoxious invasive diatom that is gaining inroads in streams on several continents! This hardy diatom is best known as "Diddymo." Diddymo takes over streams by blooming so profusely that it destroys water quality for native aquatic species. It turns out that in the laboratory, Diddymo shrinks back to manageable levels in an iron poor environment. Normally, Pactola's outlet water is drawn from high in the lake, before water has had time to settle out the majority of the natural iron it carries. Simply drawing water off the bottom of the lake will access water low in iron content. This could help solve a vexing international problem!

Most of us buy the annual National Forest user's pass for $30.00. Here are more reasons why. USFS does NOT charge for day use of the school house parking lot or the Jenney Gulch picnic area. So the best place to put-in, both for cost

DONNA SAVAGE ENJOYING JENNY GULCH

and access to calm water is at Jenney Gulch or the School House. However, the two main access points to the lake, the north and south shore boat launches charge $6.00 per vehicle per day for day use unless you have the $30.00 USFS annual day user pass. Fortunately, the USFS does not charge for day use outside of the summer season.

In spite of the stiff user fee, it is a magnificent paddle, cruising from Jenney Gulch to the dam. Paddle back to Jenney Gulch for a real workout. The round trip paddle also avoids the user fee if you don't have an annual pass on your shuttle vehicle. We recommend off–season or a cloudy, foggy or cold day, though. Try it on a sunny summer day, and you will likely have to clean out your pants after running the dam side of the lake! Even if legal right-of-way belongs to paddlers, "Stink boats" rule on the open water!

A BEAUTIFUL MORNING AT JENNY GULCH

Pactola Lake is located on US Highway 385 two miles south of the US Highway 44 junction out of Rapid City. Highway 385 runs right across the Pactola Dam with a visitor's center at the south side. The south boat launch features a picnic area, more slips for mooring, a longer less inclined boat ramp, a nice full service store, marina, modern campground and a sand beach. **Do not launch or land your boat on a marked swim beach. You will be ticketed!** The south beach campground concessionaire also operates a second private gated campground in secluded Bear Gulch, just a few miles up the lake.

We, the Black Hills Paddlers love our home lake, Pactola. We paddle it in all seasons! We paddle it all hours of the day and night, between dawn paddles, night paddles, and daytime uses. We teach on it, practice on it, race on it and relax on it. Please come join us!

29 - REAUSAW LAKE

Some Black Hills Paddlers are getting long in the tooth now. That means "old" to you younger paddlers. Elder Black Hills Paddler Kelly spent four summers teaching boating on this lake back in high school (1966-69!) Reausaw was the closest open water to the old Boy Scout Camp above Nemo. Back then to get to the lake we pulled off on the shoulder of the road. The wide spot on the shoulder is still there, but we recommend parking by the dam these days. This lake is getting old, but has a surprising amount of open water. We love the solitude of poking around in the cattails and wild rice. There is an amazing richness of biology in this lake!

REAUSAW LAKE

You get to Reausaw Lake by taking the Nemo Road all the way to Nemo, then about 3 miles past Nemo toward Deadwood. The lake is right next to the road on the south side. There are no access fees, no potable water is available and there are no services; just a lonely vault toilet on the far side of the dam.

30 - ROUBAIX LAKE

Even though the turn-off to Roubaix is well-marked along Highway 385, It always amazes us the folks who have never pulled in here. This is a *nice* sized lake with a *nice* campground and a very *nice* day use area with a *nice* beach and great water access. This is just a really *nice* lake! Paddlers will enjoy no motors, a sand beach, drinking water, vault toilets, and a picnic area. The best put-in is on either

ROUBAIX LAKE

side of the swimming area. **Do not launch or land your boat on a marked swim beach. You will be ticketed!**

Roubaix Lake camping is currently listed as no hook-ups or showers for $19.00 per night. However, the area closed to the public fall and winter of 2011-12 for what looks like a total rebuild of the camping areas, including water, sewer and power. Look for a bright, shiny new campground, perhaps with a fee increase for the summer of 2012.

Roubaix Lake was built by men of Camp F-6, Company 792 of the Civilian Conservation Corps (CCC) in the mid 1930's. There is a historical marker/plaque commemorating this accomplishment right where you turn to Roubaix Lake at the junction of Forest Road 255 and US Highway 385. Stop and at least read the sign next time you are buzzing by on 385! Get to Roubaix Lake by driving two miles past the historical marker/plaque on Forest Road 255, off of US Highway 385, about fifteen miles south of Deadwood.

31- SHERIDAN LAKE

The once-important town of Sheridan is buried beneath the waters of this, the second-largest reservoir *in* the Black Hills proper. The lake is named after the town, which was named after Army General Phillip Sheridan. This boom town hosted the first Federal Court west of the Mississippi River and was the Pennington County seat until 1887. Sheridan remained a thriving gold rush town until the turn of the century when the community found

itself left behind by the many new railroads in the Black Hills. The lure of Deadwood was too much, and Sheridan's residents drifted away. By the mid 1930's, the CCC started building a dam below the now ghost town of Sheridan.

SHERIDAN LAKE – NORTH BEACH

With looming war, the dam was completed in 1942. Beware when you paddle Sheridan Lake, you are paddling over the bones of history!

Sheridan Lake is a HEAVILY used recreation area! The lake sports the largest swim beach areas in the Black Hills **Do not launch or land your boat on a marked swim beach. You will be ticketed!** There are picnic areas near the dam, surrounding a swim beach on the southwest shore, and the north shore boasts a full service marina, including kayak rentals. The best places to launch boats are on the north shore by the marina or next to the southwest shore beach/picnic area. This lake has LOTS of powerboat traffic, but boaters can follow the shore and stay mostly in the dreaded prop grabbing water weeds and keep clear of speeding "stink boats." The headwaters of Sheridan Lake are very special to paddle boaters. The whole area seems choked with cattails. However this might as well be a clever ruse as it allows us to keep the area all to ourselves. There are myriad channels among the cattails. Just don't try to get out of your boat and stand up. Major mud lurks in those shallows!

SHERIDAN LAKE – SOUTH END

You *will* pay to play at Sheridan Lake! Unless you bought your annual Black Hills National Forest deluxe user pass for $30.00, it will cost you $6.00 per vehicle per day to use Sheridan Lake. And they *do* collect! Camping in either of two large campgrounds of course is extra. Heavy use means heavily patrolled, so license your boat if it is over 12 feet long! See the pages on licensing your lake boat toward the back of this guide.

To get to Sheridan Lake simply head between Pactola Lake and Hill City on US Highway 385. Sheridan Lake is about midway between the two. The driveway south of the lake splits to a campground or a picnic area. The driveway north of the lake is Sheridan Lake Road. It junctions right away, with the right hand fork leading to the north beach, boat launch, marina, beach day use area and a campground. The left hand fork goes on to Rapid City. About two miles down this road, look for signs accessing the dam and Dakota Point, a fairly remote picnic area and the parking area for a number of hiking trails.

32 - SLATE CREEK DAM

Slate Creek Dam is just a couple of ridges over from Silver City. Slate Creek drains into Rapid Creek which flows through Silver City and into Pactola Lake. Look up at the towering slate cliffs where this material probably came from. Notice we said *old*. Black Hills Paddlers can find no record for when Slate Creek Dam was built, but the rockwork indicates CCC workmanship from the mid-late 1930's. There is a large cattail patch at the Slate Creek input (and silt is filling in other places as well). Also note that before *old* we said *little*. This is not the place to

SLATE CREEK DAM

get a workout, but nonetheless it is a nice paddle to say you've been there. This is definitely a lake less paddled. There are no fees, no facilities, and no development. This is just a nice, little, old lake with an amazing amount of slate rock making up the rip-rapping lining the dam.

Even though it is actually closer to Silver City, the most direct way to find Slate Creek Dam is from Hill City. Take the Rochford Road out of Hill City, then the Mystic Road turn-off. Turn north at the Slate Creek Dam sign, then eight miles of gravel. The lake was drained last time we visited to paddle, but was full again by the next spring. You might see a fly fisher or a 4-wheeler when paddling, but not often. Enjoy this hidden jewel!

33 - SUNDAY GULCH POND

We watched the construction of this pond, just after the 1972 flood. We have no idea what it was originally intended for, although it is so small that any intended use other than fishing or recreation is hard to imagine. In the last few years the USFS has added a nice walkway along the south shore and dam with a couple of their very nice fishing piers. The inflow end of the lake is now deliciously overgrown. Sunday Gulch Pond is located just off of Highway 16/385 (between Hill City and Custer) and SD Highway

244 which circles the backside of Mt Rushmore. The turn-in and parking is on the north side of the lake, just ½ mile east of the junction on Hwy 244. There are no fees and no facilities except a lone porta-potty.

SUNDAY GULCH POND

34 - STOCKADE LAKE

STOCKADE LAKE – BOAT LAUNCH

The thrice rebuilt, historic, illegal Gorman Stockade that this "alpine" lake is named after now sits on a dry spot at the headwaters of Stockade Lake. The stockade is open to the public, as is the lake. Stockade Lake is the 4th largest lake *in* the Black Hills proper. It is the only one of the 4 *large* lakes, over 100 acres, in the Black Hills to lie above 6000 feet of elevation.

STOCKADE LAKE

Water quality in Stockade Lake can be delicate. The lake supports a nice cold-water fishery due to its elevation, but nutrient loading could be impacting productivity. French Creek normally provides good quality inflow for Stockade Lake, but in late season, when French Creek typically flows very little, if at all; nutrient loading increases dramatically. In this case, the only inflow for Stockade Lake is the city of Custer's treated wastewater. Even though Custer is well within its state permit standards, it still sends a nutrient–loaded inflow into Stockade Lake that is not always diluted by corresponding inflows from French Creek. Today, Stockade Lake remains a quality fishery, but it could get complicated in the future as Custer grows and conditions change.

Stockade Lake has pretty good services. The two day use areas are on the north shore, the first accessible via a dedicated driveway and the second on the east side next to the boat launch and dock. Stockade Lake also boasts two campgrounds with vault toilets, potable water and showers, one on the north, the other on the south shores ($20.00/night). The boat launch on the east end of the north shore is the best place to put in/take-out. Warning: There is a swim beach near the boat launch. **Do not launch or land your boat on a marked swim beach. You will be ticketed!** This lake does allow motorboats of all sizes so it can get busy in the summer, but usually has a fairly sleepy feel for a "stink boat" infested lake.

You can drive by Stockade Lake on US Highway 16 for free, but if you stop to paddle or play you must display a park access pass. This pass costs$14.00 per vehicle per week or $28.00 for a statewide annual pass. The $28.00 looks better than ever when you consider the number of State Park administered lakes in the Black Hills alone.

Stockade Lake is south off US Highway 16A, four miles east of Custer. It is just inside the western-most Custer State Park entrance. Three driveways access the lake. The boat launch is about a mile down the eastern-most lake-drive road.

35 - SYLVAN LAKE

Sylvan means surrounded by or contained within a grove of trees. Somehow, Sylvan Lake epitomizes the whole concept of a beautiful mountain lake closely surrounded by giant trees. The jumble of rocks around most of the lake is reminiscent of the BWCA wilderness in Northern Minnesota and Canada. There are reason's paddling Sylvan Lake seems so magical. Sylvan Lake was built in 1881 when Theodore Reder first put a dam across Sunday Gulch.

It is the oldest reservoir in the Black Hills. The water quality in this lake is excellent. There is a sand beach and swimming area on the north shore Warning: **Do not launch or land your boat on a marked swim beach. You will be ticketed!**

Even when the place is swarming with visitors, things become very calm as soon as you put-in. The best put-in/take out is about halfway down the road to the Sylvan Lake Picnic Ground/ Harney Peak trailhead. There is a nice sandy spot to pull off, unload your boat and slide it into the water. Beware: Parking can be just about impossible mid-days during the summer. Plan your put-in/ take-out times accordingly. This is a popular destination for visitors and locals alike. There is NO camping around Sylvan Lake except for camping cabins operated by Sylvan Lake Resort. What is now the picnic area and Harney Peak trailhead parking used to be the campground, but SDGFP gave up on the crowds 30 years ago and relocated the campground about a mile further down Highway 87. There are lots of services available at the south end of Sylvan Lake. Sylvan Lake Lodge is perched above the lake. Architect Frank Lloyd Wright redesigned the *new* Sylvan Lake Lodge on top of the ridge two years after the original Lodge on the Lake's shore was incinerated in 1935.

The "new" Sylvan Lake Lodge offers character, ambiance, and wonderful food, for a price. Below the Lodge, Sylvan Lake Resort offers a nice gift shop, convenience store, and a lunch counter with a view of the Lake. Sylvan Lake Resort even has paddle boats and rec kayaks/canoes that you can rent. Sylvan Lake also offers walking trails around the lake. Potable water and flush toilets available at the north side picnic ground/ Harney Peak trailhead.

SYLVAN LAKE – BOAT LAUNCH

If you haven't yet purchased your annual entrance sticker for SD State Parks yet, this is a good time to do that. You must pass through the manned entrance station to get to Sylvan Lake. $28.00 for a year's entrance to all SDGFP facilities, or $14.00 for one week?

To get there: drive to Custer State Park. Hill City is the closest town, but you can drive to Custer State Park via Hill City, Keystone, Custer or Hermosa. Sylvan Lake is in Custer State Park on SD Highway 87 about ¼ mile past the intersection of SD Highways 87 and 89.

PADDLING RIVERS AND STREAMS OF THE
BLACK HILLS

The Black Hills receive 14-17 inches of moisture annually. Barring rampant global warming, that isn't enough water to bathe in year-round, much less float a boat. To be a creek boater in the Black Hills you just have to time it right. The United States Geological Survey (USGS) is the boater's best friend. They have set up monitoring stations on eight different drainages in the Black Hills. Here is a link to our favorite USGS page. http://waterwatch.usgs.gov/new/?m=real&r=sd&w=real%2Ctable_flow

Look around the website for a page configuration that best suits your information needs. If you know how to apply the USGS website's data to the section of creek you want to paddle, then you can be on playable moving water within an hour's drive of Rapid City, from March through October.

This section of the paddle guide is a creek-by-creek look at 33 paddle-able routes in the Black Hills with flow estimates based on USGS data from these eight drainages, plus an addendum afterwards for water routes that have been paddled, but mostly are not paddled at the present, for whatever reason. We give you some river "beta," or information, about the paddle's difficulties, hazards, length, shuttling from put-in to take-out, and even some fun history and anecdotes. See the last chapter of this guide for more information including things like American Whitewater's (AW) description of the International Class rating system. Streams are listed by common name, from north to south as they exit the Black Hills. Individual runs are listed from top to bottom for each stream.

Although there is a lot of information in this document, it is a paddling guide, not a tutorial. Black Hills Paddlers presumes you have or have access to appropriate boats for the water you want to paddle and the essential gear and skills necessary to safely navigate runs you choose on our Black Hills streams.

PPPPPP – PRIOR PLANNING PREVENTS PISS-POOR PERFORMANCE
Excellent advice from iconic backcountry adventurer and
NOLS founder, Paul Petzolt

SAFETY WHEN PADDLING BLACK HILLS STREAMS

With spring rains, many local creeks and rivers run high or near flood stage. This is especially so in our Black Hills where the geography encourages run-off. The Black Hills paddle sports community reminds canoeists and kayakers to paddle safely. Consider stream conditions before starting out. Some important safety tips:

- If you're not prepared, stay out of the water!
- Engage your brain "before" getting on the water.
- Never paddle moving water alone; EVER!
- If ANYONE in your group is uncomfortable with stream level or conditions, at any time, get off the water.

- Paddlers love a beer or a drink, AFTER paddling! They know impaired judgment is an open invite for bad decisions on the water with potentially disastrous consequences!
- Know your route's hazards: If you haven't paddled the route before, do some homework. High water is not a good time to start. What are estimated time to paddle, known problems, max safe flow, locations of safe put-ins and take-outs?
- Ask a local for guidance and advice. Members of Black Hills Paddlers will gladly show you our favorite routes, and probably even come paddle with you.
- Be sure to respect private property and landowner's rights. A friendly and polite demeanor goes a long way when trouble happens and you need a local hand.
- "If in doubt, scout!" Know what is around the next corner "this second" or stop to find out.
- Respect the power of moving water, especially at high flows.
- Cold water affects your motor skills, coordination and JUDGEMENT even when air temps are in the 80's.
- Have and practice the skills, knowledge and experience to SAFELY navigate hazards before paddling anywhere.
- Have and know how to use proper safety gear.

STREAM RATINGS AND DIFFICULTY

We consciously choose not to limit our ratings of individual creeks to the AW whitewater rating scale. By and large nearly all of these Black Hills runs are easy Class I to Class II with an occasional Class III drop, depending upon flows. There are problem spots on some sections, which we do note as we become aware of them. The full AWA whitewater rating scale is included in the final section of this guide, Other Essential Paddle Information for your reference. Why this decision to avoid hard and fast labels?

REASON #1: Stream flows hugely affect paddling conditions in our usually little creeks. The Black Hills offers mostly narrow streams. They are NOT big water. A desirable flow for most Black Hills streams is 100 to 300 cubic feet/second (CFS.) As with any guideline, there are exceptions to these flows. For example, Sand Creek is a lot of fun at 25 CFS which seems too low to be possible. At the other end, Rapid Creek through Dark Canyon is probably safest (for skilled boaters who are not likely to swim) at 300 CFS. Some parts of the Cheyenne River are too low to paddle under 400 CFS. Generally, safe flow for beginners on a given run is significantly less than for more experienced, better equipped boaters. When the water is big in the Hills, meaning around 400+ CFS, the banks run full. This pushes a kayak around much more so than a big drop on say, Colorado's Poudre River where higher flows are normal and the stream bed is so much more accommodating.

REASON #2: Strainers, like downed trees which block your paddle line and can 'strain out' a paddler, are constant problems in our streams. A single tree is more than capable of blocking most Black Hills streams, creating a deadly strainer. Ponder this: a single cubic foot of water weighs more than your boat (62.5 lb.) Multiply that by the cubic feet per second (CFS) you are paddling in, then flip in the creek and hit your head on a rock, or get pinned against a big tree trunk with HOW MUCH force pushing you against an immovable object and what is the result? The fact that Black Hills streams have evolved to flush straight out of the Hills makes their flows highly variable. A class 2 rapid in low water could become a potential killer class 4 at high water!

REASON #3: The one thing we can promise you: You will see a new creek, river or lake every time you paddle in our beautiful Black Hills. Be ready, paddle safe. Portage or stay off the water if you get surprised, by any conditions!

STREAM PADDLING ETIQUETTE AND THE LAW

Whether you are a grizzled old "creeker" or brand new paddler, please remember: we do not paddle in a vacuum. ENGAGE YOUR BRAIN before paddling! Traditionally, boaters have been allowed to paddle any water that flows out of the Black Hills.

According to South Dakota law, navigable rivers and streams are public highways. Landowners cannot stop you passing through their land on navigable streams in South Dakota. However, legally, you must stay in the water or within the normal high water flood line.

The term "navigable" was narrowly defined in 1990. Navigable rivers and streams are designated by the South Dakota Legislature as being capable of supporting/floating a manned canoe or other vessel throughout the summer in at least two out of every ten years. The "list" of navigable streams in Western South Dakota includes parts of the Cheyenne and Red Water Rivers only.

What about all the other streams we like to run? There are a lot, to us at least, of paddle-able streams flowing out of the Black Hills that we find navigable, but are not on the list! What does this mean? It is a very grey area, we fear. The intent of the 1990 legislation was to clarify fencing of rivers on the prairie for livestock management, not to deny recreational access to paddlers.

The letter of the law does bring into question the right of recreational users to be on non-navigable waters at all. Case law supports recreational use of any paddle-able waiter in South Dakota within the high water line without trespass. This includes the right to walk around fences if necessary without trespass. It falls back on us as responsible paddlers to be as respectful of private property as possible.

The South Dakota Department of Environment and Natural Resources has published a booklet regarding stream navigability and landowner rights regarding fences. It is available on their website at:
www.state.sd.us/denr/des/waterrights/StreamFencingGuide.pdf

All of the streams flowing out of the Black Hills flow through some private property. Paddlers in the Black Hills by and large get along well with non-paddling recreation users and landowners. This could be because there aren't a lot of us, and we want to believe paddlers make as small a footprint as possible when passing through backyards or private creek-fronts which landowners appreciate. Please, please, please, continue to respect landowner rights! Let's continue to minimize our impact. "Leave No Trace" physically or verbally. We suggest these guidelines:

1. Pack out what you pack in! Leave no trace.

2. Respect other recreational users on the water.

3. Plan ahead for put-in and take-out parking for your favorite creek, stream or river. Even if it's not as convenient, find an out-of-the-way, legal place to park your shuttle. Many of us shuttle shorter distances with mountain bikes or small dirt bikes to minimize this. Most paddlers also develop a network of places to park on favorite runs, often by building a network of property owners giving them permission to park. This is one of the many reasons you should contact local paddlers if you are new or just visiting the Black Hills

4. Even with permission to park, do not block driveways, side roads, equipment access, leave vehicles in picnic areas overnight, etc.!

5. Beyond parking, just accessing waterways in the west can be touchy. The streams that get paddled regularly generally do not have fences across them and all parties acknowledge that recreational users of the water can pass through private property so long as they stay within the high water marks of the stream. This means you must plan ahead where to put-in, take-out or in choosing a bank to eat your lunch on.

6. In high water years, there are usually several new streams having enough water to be paddle-able for the first time in a long time. Many of these irregularly paddled streams are fenced for livestock. DO NOT CUT FENCES! Trust us, in spite of what you believe is right, this is ILLEGAL! You WILL be prosecuted, and you SHOULD be prosecuted! Scout, then portage as needed! Landowner and recreational users each have some responsibilities and some rights. Cutting a fence is not among them! This creates a huge liability if livestock gets loose and cause other property damage or a vehicle collision. Those fences are there for a reason, like it or not. Many fences can easily be slipped under or you can lift your boat over them. Others, yes, you must portage around. Many landowners we have talked to are willing to work with paddlers to make their fences passable to kayaks and still contain livestock. Most landowners actually enjoy watching us paddle through their backyards. They think our bright boats and colorful gear is cool! More than a few would like to paddle with us! Please pass through politely! You're an ambassador, not an invader! We

have personally had very positive experiences with landowners on the Red Water, Cheyenne, Belle Fourche and Missouri Rivers, Rapid Creek, Spearfish Creek, Sand Creek, and Box Elder Creek.

7. In an emergency, everything changes. Good Samaritan laws kick in. South Dakotans are inherently helpful in bad times, so don't be afraid to ask if you really need a hand. Please, try not to give folks a reason to not be friendly and helpful.

8. If you do encounter a mess or rudeness, know your rights and be polite. You might be cleaning up from an irresponsible paddler. This is a good chance to do some "fence mending!"

KELLY ON SPEARFISH CREEK

PADDLE TO LIVE

LIVE TO PADDLE!

DRAINAGE 1 – SAND CREEK

SAND CREEK PUBLIC FISHING AREA

Sand Creek is actually in the Wyoming Black Hills, so leave your fishing pole at home if you are from South Dakota (This is an outstanding fishing

SAND CREEK PUT-IN

stream if you do have a Wyoming license!). The preferred run on Sand Creek is through the public access area just below the housing development. Resident paddlers have blanket permission to paddle through the housing area, but the run through the public access area is still plenty of fun: 2 1/2 hours, very short shuttle and no one is ragging you all the way down to prove you have permission to be there.

It is a bit of a drive to get to Sand Creek. From South Dakota, get on I-90 and drive to Wyoming. Take the first Wyoming exit at Beulah. There is a nice convenience store here, but to get to Sand Creek turn south away from Beulah. About three to four miles down the road you pass three access roads with brown USFS signs (Actually they are Wyoming Fish and Game signs). Take the third access road (right turn to the creek) closest to the first house on the left (housing development caretaker's house).

CHRIS SURFS A WAVE ON SAND CREEK

The road ends at the creek! Shuttle goes just a mile back to the first public access road. We typically park by the outhouse.

Now the fun begins. We often call Sand Creek our "teaching creek" because this creek itself demands almost nothing from paddlers at the

JONATHAN HUFT RUNS THE BIG DROP ON SAND CREEK

beginning. Begin your paddle by launching your boat from the shore into Sand Creek. The deeply cut banks up here really call for a seal launch, which is where you slide off the top of the bank into the water. If you are not ready for that you can walk upstream a hundred feet and get in your

DONNA ON SAND CREEK

boat from water level. Follow the gentle meander downstream. You could hardly even call the stream Class I at the start of this run. There are, however 25 drops on this creek of 18 inches or more! And, conveniently, they pretty much come in order of difficulty. Little by little, as a new boater's confidence improves, the creek asks a bit more, and a bit more. By the end of the run boaters have shot a double four foot drop, seven foot waterfall and a respectable Class II drop with Class III turns on it.

CHAD & BEN PLAY ON SAND CREEK

Experienced (and old) boaters love this creek just as much, if not more than beginners. Sand Creek is just plain beautiful as it meanders along. One of the few downsides; there is a ton of poison ivy along the creek. Be mindful of this pesky plant. The poison ivy is offset by crystal clear spring water, incredible fish, wildlife and wildflowers. Sand Creek is paddleable nearly all year. A growing number of paddlers have personally paddled it in every month except December and January. Being spring-fed means Sand Creek has unbelievably steady flows.

We think it is very paddle-able from 24 cubic feet per second (CFS) on up. We've never seen it too high to paddle. This beautiful, but narrow, meandering creek is best paddled in a whitewater boat with a skirt, not for difficulty, but for easier surfing and turning. There are a couple

CHAD, MIKE & JUSTIN ON SAND CREEK

of decent play waves if you have the boat for it. Many folks have paddled Sand Creek in up to 12 foot rec boats, though. If you do paddle a longer boat, be careful about pitch-poling and rolling over on the seven foot waterfall with such a long boat. Like the whole creek, even this drop is more fun than dangerous. Still, we always spot this and the last rapid for new boaters. It's just a good habit. As mentioned above it is usually about a 2+ hour paddle, so, with the 1 hour drive each way from, say Rapid City, 1 hour to gear up, set shuttle, then load back up, give yourself at least 7 hours for this run. That doesn't count the time to stop in Spearfish for a cold one at Crow Peak Brewery if you are so inclined! It is best if you just plan to make a day of this trip.

Sand Creek to Beulah

When Dan Crain first paddled Sand Creek all the way to its confluence with the Red Water River North of Beulah, he said it wasn't worth the work. At low flows, it isn't. There are fences, switchbacks, strainers, boney rapids, and way too many portages! Black Hills Paddlers discovered, quite by accident, that this run is worth it at higher flows. In the spring of 2011, a heavy front settled over the Sand Creek drainage off and on, for over a week. Where normal flow on Sand Creek is 25 - 45 CFS, Mike Ray and Scotty Nelson found themselves at the takeout that day, watching 75 CFS of water flow on downstream. On a whim, they continued downstream to Beulah, about another hour of paddling with nearly all obstacles safely submerged. Mike and Scotty got out at Beulah bar rather than going all the way out to the Sand Creek, Red water confluence. The locals at the Beulah bar sure gave them a load of it when they saw their

EDITOR'S NOTE: This lower section of Sand Creek is not a recommended run. In the spring of 2012 Black Hills Paddlers stopped by the rancher's house and asked the landowner about access. We were told access is preferential for fishing and not for boating. We were asked to keep boating contained to the upper section of the creek above the sign. Good stewardship of this resource would suggest we respect the landowner's wishes.

colorful paddle jackets, pfd's and boats!! High flow on Sand Creek is over 70 CFS. The highest flow we have paddled on Sand Creek is 181 CFS, which is pushy, but oh, so much fun!

Sand Creek - Wyoming

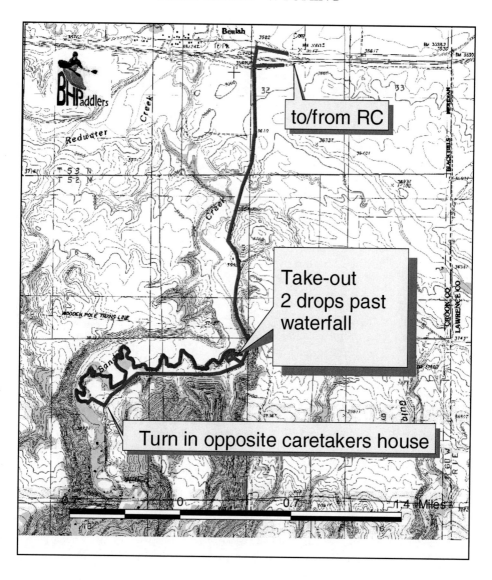

Drainage 2 - Red Water River

This is a great starter river. It barely even goes Class II anywhere, but the upper part of the river is fickle at best. The middle section (Highway 85 bridge down) is much more boater friendly! There are a few easy rapids and an occasional play wave.

Beulah to McNenny Road Bridge

When the Red Water first becomes run able near Beulah, it becomes much like sand creek with lots of downed trees. Even if you break up the trip at the McNenny Road bridge, few paddlers have endurance for the run from its Sand Creek confluence down to the Highway 85 bridge. Spearfish creek has not yet added its flow and it has too much wire fencing on it, along with huge strainers. For the simple limitations of logistics, and the reality that Sand creek only feeds enough flow to the Red water early in the season when the water is really cold, Black Hills Paddlers doesn't recommend this run without a lot of support and planning, and patience! Kayaking mentor Dan Crain wrote this description on his website (now long taken down):

“ The Redwater River begins its journey in the Bear Lodge Mountains of Wyoming, runs eastward and joins forces with the much larger Sand Creek in Beulah, Wyoming. After this merger with Sand Creek the Redwater becomes run able. The section from Beulah to the bridge over the river, north of McNenny Fish Hatchery takes most people around 6 hours to run. Plan on a full day. The character of this section is a small meandering stream, many overhanging trees and strainers to maneuver around. There are a few small rapids in the Class I + range. The main hazards are trees and a few fences. It is a very enjoyable stretch of water, numerous muskrats, deer, birdlife, and small ranches. For a shorter trip (1 hour) take out at the bridge north of Beulah. ”

McNenny Road Bridge to Highway 85 Bridge

Our mentor, Dan Crain managed this dawn to dusk slog just once. Likely doable by mere mortals at high flows (minimum 75 CFS at Beulah, 300CFS+ by the Highway 85 bridge.) but not recommended! Dan says:

“If you put on at the bridge north of McNenny Fish Hatchery and are planning to take out at the Highway 85 Bridge; plan on a very long day. A good rule of thumb for the Redwater is: for every mile that you drive on the roads that parallel the river plan on 1 hour on the water. This section takes about 10 hours on the water. It is Class I to I+ in nature and major hazards are strainers and fences. ”

HIGHWAY 85 BRIDGE TO PEPIN RANCH

Here is what Dan says about the Redwater River further downstream:

" The section most commonly run and the section that I recommend for your first taste of the Redwater is the Highway 85 Bridge to Pepin's Ranch. The volume of water has doubled thanks to Spearfish Creek, which comes in a mile or so upstream of the bridge. As of 10-6-02, there are no strainers and no fences, nice easy rapids and beginner surf waves. I always see muskrat, lots of fish, and on occasion you'll see huge snapping turtles. You'll paddle past South Dakota's version of Car-henge. The farmers and ranchers of the area in a few spots have used old cars to stop stream bank erosion. Not the best choice of materials, but in the day an inexpensive solution to losing farm land. This section takes 1 hour if you paddle hard and don't stop to play, or up to 4 hours if you like surfing, eddy line cartwheels, and squirting. Generally it's about 2 hours on the water. To get to the take out head back towards Spearfish about 300 yards take a left on Hardin dirt road, go 2 miles and take another left on Lookout Mt. Road, proceed another 1/2 mile to the bridge. Park your vehicle under the tree way off the road so the farmers can get their equipment past. Better yet, cross over the bridge and park between Mr. Pepin's mailbox and the corrals. He told me he actually prefers you to park on his land, but also that he wants you to ask permission as well. "

REDWATER RIVER – OLD HIGHWAY 16 PUT-IN

The preferred put-in is the Highway 85 Bridge. For an alternative put-in, go to the next bridge upstream (old Highway 16) which is less than a mile west, but adds half a river mile (about 45 minutes) to the run. DO NOT try and put in further upstream than the old

Highway 16 bridge due to slow water flow, and way too many fences and strainers. This section is often not even passable except during high water. Caution, if you get confused and put in on Spearfish creek before it meets the Red Water there are several dangerous and potentially deadly low head dams!

We try to talk each year to Mr. Pepin, the owner of the ranch at the county road bridge. He welcomes paddlers, reminding them to park in the yard over by the corrals. Don't block the county road if any equipment needs to get by. Knock on the door and say hi and thank you. Someone is usually home. His ranch is right at the only county bridge midway between the US Highway 85 bridge and the US Highway 34 bridge.

PEPIN RANCH TO HIGHWAY 34 BRIDGE

If you want to go further, stay in the water and paddle to the next highway bridge. Black Hills Paddler Leroy Henderson especially likes the run below the Pepin Ranch to the Highway 34 bridge. It's the same easy river, and about another hour and a

REDWATER RIVER

half to the Highway 34 bridge. This is US Highway 34 between St. Onge and Belle Fourche. There is a campground on the downstream side of the highway bridge that welcomes paddlers. For $5.00 you can park on campground property right next to the river for a very convenient take-out and not worry about your vehicle. You probably do not want to go further without some planning, but this is also a nice place to leave a shuttle vehicle for the lower section of the river.

HIGHWAY 34 BRIDGE TO RIVER CONFLUENCE IN BELLE FOURCHE

Put in and leave your vehicle secure at river's edge after self-paying $5.00 at the campsite downstream of the bridge. From here to Belle Fourche City and the Red Water's confluence with the Belle Fourche River is another winding, half day of paddling. It takes three hours at high flows (600 CFS) and there are lots of potential strainers. Last time down, we had to portage two strainers and slip past one more. Take-out is problematic as the river cuts deeper and deeper into the surrounding bluffs and sand/clay cliffs. There is a lack of public access until you get into Belle Fourche. We paddled all three sections of the Red Water from the US Highway 85 bridge to Belle Fourche recently and all three sections had strainers, big enough that we had to get out and portage. At high flows these strainers come up quick so be aware and prepared!

EDITOR'S NOTE: We elected not to include Keyhole Reservoir as a Black Hills lake because it is upstream of any drainage from the Black Hills or Bear lodge Mountains. Orman Dam also controls a large part of Keyhole Reservoir's water. Now if we could just get some advance notice of WHEN Orman calls for a big release from Keyhole and ride that wave?!

A bit of history: Three miles upstream from Belle Fourche you paddle under an obviously historical bridge. This is the Minesela Bridge, marking the location of the ghost town of Minesela (Lakota for "Red water"). Minesela was once a thriving town alongside the Red Water River until it was out-maneuvered for the vital railroad contract by Deadwood's Seth

TYPICAL REDWATER RIVER "RAPIDS"

Bullock whose ranch at the confluence of two rivers grew into today's Belle Fourche. Early French-speaking trappers and traders spoke fondly of a beautiful fork, or belle fourche where two rivers met.

Watch out for some powerful eddies as the Red Water River rushes in to mix at this "beautiful fork" of the Red Water and Belle Fourche Rivers. This is the most convenient spot to take-out. There is a flight of stairs that leads to the Riverside Campground and RV Park right at the confluence. We are told we can park at the river edge of the campground for free, but at least offer to pay! Access to either the Belle Fourche or the Red Water River with the very high steep banks really is a problem. When you spot this stairway up the bank it will seem like a prayer answered. Most of the year the Red Water contributes more in-flow to the confluence than the rather anemic Belle Fourche River usually contributes. During spring flood, though, watch out! The Belle Fourche River drains a lot of the Northern Black Hills and when it floods, it floods good!

REDWATER RIVER

Drainage 3 - Belle Fourche River

Relatively few people paddle the Belle Fourche River. There are occasional fences across the river in its entire upper length. In the spring, or when Keyhole Reservoir releases water, it should be possible to paddle the Belle Fourche River out of Keyhole Reservoir, past Devil's Tower and on into Belle Fourche or beyond. We know of folks who have paddled bits and pieces of this upper river, but not enough to say there is an established route on it.

Belle Fourche River Sand Bar Lunch Stop

Flows in the Belle Fourche River have been very solidly consistent in recent years, especially downstream of the city of Belle Fourche, due to the Belle Fourche River's confluence with the Red Water River right in Belle Fourche.

WARNING

BELLE FOURCHE RIVER DIVERSION DAM

If you plan on paddling through Belle Fourche City you MUST take-out of the river no later than the First US Highway 212 Bridge east of Belle Fourche City! There is a **DEADLY** diversion dam just downstream of here and the river is closed to recreational use here due to the hazard which has caused multiple fatalities. The easiest place to put-in below Belle Fourche City is 6 miles east of town at the second US Highway 212 bridge over the Belle Fourche River.

This dam that is not a dam is part of our consideration of both streams and lakes in the Black Hills because the Belle Fourche diversion dam is a deadly hazard on the Belle Fourche River and it is also called a dam, which could mislead paddlers not familiar with the area. **This is no place for paddlers!** This diversion dam is not a dam in the sense of a water impoundment. It is the junction where the Bureau of Reclamation diverts water from the Belle Fourche River through a 6 mile long diversion ditch to feed the Belle Fourche Reservoir, also known as

DIVERSION DAM

Orman Dam. Orman Dam is the impoundment damming neighboring Crow Creek Valley. The upstream diversion dam diverts water from the Belle Fourche River into Crow Creek Valley where it becomes the Belle Fourche River water storage reservoir for the Bureau of Reclamation's very ambitious Belle Fourche Irrigation project.

This diversion dam is **DEADLY TO PADDLERS**. On older maps this is listed as a dam because at one point in time there was an impoundment of water at the diversion site. Unfortunately, that impoundment area is now silted in and paddlers are funneled straight through the big gates with deadly

BELLE FOURCHE RIVER CLOSURE SIGN

recirculating hydraulics. These hydraulics are the unfortunate site of a triple fatality summer of 2010. The Diversion dam section of The Belle Fourche River is now **CLOSED TO RIVER USERS!** From upstream we recommend a very nice take-out at City Park in the center of Belle Fourche City. Put in where the Belle Fourche River crosses Highway 212 DOWNSTREAM (east) of the reservoir. *NOTE* This put-in is the second place the river crosses Highway 212 east of Belle Fourche City. DO NOT try and put in where the River crosses Highway 212 east of town for the first time, just east of town. You are a short mile upstream of the diversion dam! This should be well signed, but just in case: Stay Out!

BELLE FOURCHE RIVER

It raises an odd question why the Irrigation water going into the Belle Fourche Reservoir must travel from the diversion dam so many miles upstream? The answer is geography. In order to get any slope for water to move from the river to the reservoir, it had to come from 6+ miles upstream. The slope on the intake canal from river to reservoir is just 0.0002; in degrees, 0.11 . That's not whitewater!

Downstream of Belle Fourche, there are fewer fences. The Belle Fourche River is also too wide from here down for most strainers to block the entire river. However, the Belle Fourche River meanders like crazy and cuts deep into its banks. We hate to admit it, but it is kind of boring. However, with increasing numbers of recreational boaters, use will likely increase.

There is also a potential health hazard lurking in the deeply cut banks of the Belle Fourche River beginning just upstream of the US Highway 79 Bridge over the Belle Fourche River about three miles south of the US Highway 79 junction with US Highway 212. This is less than a half-mile below where Whitewood Creek joins the Belle Fourche River. From 1876 - 1977 Whitewood Creek was a virtual cesspool of toxic mine waste and human effluent. From a paddlers viewpoint there was NO fish life and NO bottom dwelling macroinvertebrates surviving in the stream. Silt from mine tailings was deposited along the banks of Whitewood Creek in waves up to 15 feet high. The 18 miles of this, now mitigated, EPA superfund site ends at Whitewood Creek's confluence with the Belle Fourche River. The streambed and water of Whitewood creek are now beautiful and healthy, but what of the stream banks? Researchers still find significant levels of toxic chemicals (arsenic) in silt deposits along Whitewood Creek, down the Belle Fourche River and on into the Cheyenne and Missouri rivers.

BELLE FOURCHE RIVER MUD FLATS

Modern medicine has given us increasing awareness of the effect of chemicals on hormone disruption in humans. Paddling this bit of the Belle Fourche River just downstream of a Superfund Site could be questionable, especially if you are chemically sensitive or planning a pregnancy?

ALKALI ROAD TO NEW UNDERWOOD ROAD

CHUCK ON THE BELLE FOURCHE RIVER

There are two relatively short, 12 and 18 river miles respectively, sections of the Belle Fourche River, starting at the top of the above run. The first is from the bridge on the Hereford road (County Road 12) to the bridge on the New Underwood road (County Road 21). Black Hills paddlers Chuck and Leroy report this run to take about four hours at low flows (300CFS) and there is no wire! This run is doable most of the summer. Very short shuttle: Drop off pick-up vehicle at bridge north of New Underwood (Hereford). Go north one mile, then west on Hereford Road to next bridge over river for put-in. Don't get dizzy with all the big meanders in the river!

NEW UNDERWOOD ROAD TO ELM SPRINGS BRIDGE

The second run is between the Hereford and Elm Springs Bridges. Put-in at Hereford Bridge straight north of New Underwood. Take-out at Elm Springs Bridge. Shuttle is short. Go two miles back south on New Underwood Road, ten miles east on West Elm Springs Road (County Road 6), then

BELLE FOURCHE RIVER

north on Elm Springs Road to bridge. It's a 45 minute shuttle and takes three hours each run, up seven hours for both runs at average mid-summer flows (300+ CFS). We've never seen more than a couple of single strand fences across it. The river meanders through some nice breaks. These are two great little runs to see how you like our prairie rivers.

NEW UNDERWOOD ROAD OR ELM SPRINGS BRIDGE TO HWY 34 BRIDGE VIA BELLE FOURCHE/ CHEYENNE RIVERS CONFLUENCE

A personal favorite run on the Belle Fourche River is a combination Belle Fourche/ Cheyenne River run from Hereford or Elm Springs bridges to the Four Corners Bridge. This route is nearly 50 river miles and is best undertaken as an overnight trip, putting in below Hereford which is straight north of New Underwood. You will have just a few fences from here to the Cheyenne. Usually all you find is single strand, although

BELLE FOURCHE RIVER

sometimes the single strand is electric. Usually a boater can lift the wire up with their paddle and slip under; just be aware! The confluence of the two rivers is quite spectacular. The leftovers from flooding after spring flows give the land a moonscape-like feeling. Read the section on the Cheyenne River for more general tips. For best takeout go one mile past the old Four Corners bridge to the main Highway 34/73 bridge. Take out under the bridge. The tiny village of Bridger is also at this junction (no store, no services, and no good place to park a shuttle.) Nearest services are at Howes Corner about five miles north back up Highway 34. For driving to the take-out, we think it easier to just go north of either Hereford or Elm Springs to Highway 34, then East to Howes Corner and follow Highway 34 as it curves down to the bridge. Be prepared, it's two-plus hours each way!

Drainage 4 - Spearfish Creek

Spearfish Creek Through The Town Of Spearfish

Spearfish Creek through the town of Spearfish was THE favorite of Black Hills Paddlers mentors, Dan Crain and Todd Andrew. Both of these outstanding boaters learned to paddle on this run. Both men lived and owned businesses in Spearfish. The two would tether themselves to the footbridge at their takeout point to perfect their rolls. Although a large flood in about 2006 scoured the creek bed and changed some of its characteristics, Dan's description of the run is still the standard:

" Spearfish Creek is a clear stream that runs through the town of Spearfish. The creek used to flow freely but in the early part of the 20th century, Homestake Gold mine built a series of low head dams to control the creek for the production of electricity. Today, all but one mile of the twenty miles of Spearfish Canyon is partly or totally dewatered. With the closing of Homestake in 2002 renewed efforts are underway to remove the dams. Time will tell.

The section that most people run on the creek is from the D.C. Booth Fish Hatchery in the city park down to Evans Park off of Lower Valley Road.

Whether it be the expert kayaker playing their way down, doing eddy-line cartwheels and splatwheels, or the beginner, full of adrenaline, worried about the falls in the park or swimming the S-turns, Spearfish Creek has a lot to offer for water in the Black Hills: year round flows, easy access and it's in my home town. You can bang your way down in January at 50 CFS if you really need to get wet or throw down in the massive ledge hole that forms during a June thunderstorm.

At 80 feet per mile, the action on Spearfish Creek is continuous Class II. Beginners' big smiles and wild talk about the rapids testify to the adrenaline rush just delivered and experts in low volume play boats can find enough play to get a good workout. The Third Street eddyline offers a great place to tune up your flat water skills. The low head dam just above Utah St. bridge has brought smiles to many and swims to others which also brought smiles to many more. There are numerous splat rocks, a few deep eddylines, and the ever popular lawn splat spots that dot the creek side.

During the hot summer months you'll share the creek with local kids in inner tubes. During the dead of winter only a few die hard locals with a serious need to get wet will be found.

Class II paddlers will want to be aware of the "Falls," a 4' cascading drop in the city park. It generally doesn't cause too much to worry about. It gives beginners wide eyes, but I've never seen anyone swim because of it. Just downstream of the falls, maybe 100 yards, is a nice beginner surf wave formed by a piece of concrete. Another 75 yards or so and you'll be at the S-turns. This little rapid causes more swims than any other place on the creek. You'll want to avoid the river-right rock towards the bottom of the rapid.

Wood can be a problem on the creek at times, so be alert. The new Nash St. bridge may cause problems during times of high water. At normal flows you'll have about 3' of clearance under the bridge. If the water is muddy please inspect this bridge before getting in as there are no good eddies above it. Wood tends to collect here and it would not be a good place to be. Below Utah bridge and just past the geodesic dome home is another rapid of concern - Squeeze play. As the creek turns and winds its way among the willows it picks up speed and squeezes down to about 6' wide. A few more drops add to the excitement just after the squeeze. Continue on down a couple of hundred yards to the take out on river-left just above the barbed wire fence that blocks your passage. Look for the wide concrete path that leads to Evans Park.

To find the put-in, take exit 12 off of I-90 and head down into town on Jackson Street. Proceed to the second light and turn left on Canyon Street. Follow Canyon through the stop signs and into the city park and park on the right just before the bridge.

To find the take-out, take exit 12 off of I-90 and proceed downhill on Jackson. Cross over the creek and through the next light and turn right on St. Joe just past the Dodge Dealership. Follow St. Joe about 2 miles, turn right on Custer St. in the new Evans subdivision. Follow Custer St. around to Evans Park.

Don't forget Guinness on tap at Knights Cellar. **"**

Well said! Thanks, Dan!!

EDITOR'S NOTE: Our current preferred watering hole has since migrated a bit north to Crow Peak Brewery

SPEARFISH CREEK – TOWN SECTION

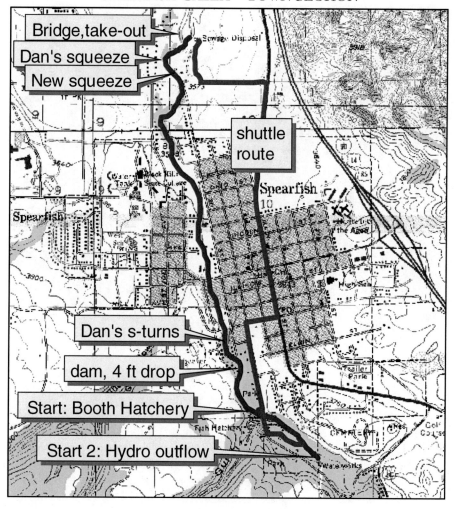

Bridge, take-out

Dan's squeeze

New squeeze

shuttle route

Dan's s-turns

dam, 4 ft drop

Start: Booth Hatchery

Start 2: Hydro outflow

LOWER SPEARFISH CANYON

This is an exciting new section of Creek that pioneering paddlers in our area, Dan Crain, Todd Andrew, and Andrew Hentz worked on getting flows restored to for years. Their goal was to get natural water flows restored to all of this historic canyon. In a kind of 50/50, win/win deal several miles of creek have now been restored to native flows, while flows through town are protected as well.

THE TEN EYCK BROTHERS AT HYDRO PLANT #2

Homestake Mine was sold to the State of South Dakota in 2002, and large-scale mining ceased. The mine itself is beginning a new phase in its history as an underground science laboratory. However, with the end of large scale mining, there was no longer the need for power generation capacity from two hydro plants that required the entire normal flow of Spearfish Canyon to run. As a result, Homestake permanently shut down Hydro Plant #1 and native flow was restored to the section of Spearfish Canyon right below Savoy late in 2003. The City of Spearfish then bought Hydro Plant #2 and operates it today. With the intake five miles upstream at Maurice diverting nearly the creek's entire flow to the Plant just above Spearfish City, this would seem counterproductive. However, there is some professional concern that the restored flow would disappear into the porous limestone that appears in the lower canyon floor just upstream of Hydro Plant #2 above Spearfish City. By virtue of some pretty unusual logic, part of the Canyon from Savoy to Maurice is paddle-able in summer because Hydro Plant 1 is shut down, while Spearfish Creek through town still enjoys reliable flows, possibly because Hydro Plant 2 still runs.

Water in the restored section of the Spearfish Canyon is still a new concept. The three sections (upper, middle and lower) that the Black Hills Paddlers have divided the Canyon into have still only been paddled a few times each. The upper third was first paddled in 2010 by Leroy, Justin, Ben, Chris, and Mike. The middle section of the restored canyon is considered Class III - IV with a lot of technical moves and needs just the right flows! The lower third of the restored canyon looks challenging but with a good roll, attention to wood and flows, is a lot of fun! Caleb and Ryan Ten Eyck get first descent on these two sections in 2008.

Mike Ray, one of a new generation of paddlers embarrassing us old guys, really likes this section of Spearfish Creek. Here is what Mike has to say:

" It should be noted that there are no USGS stream gauges above the city of Spearfish, so all flows listed here are based on the reading at the stream gauge in Spearfish. This gauge may not represent the actual flow in the canyon, but it makes for a good reference point. "

MIKE RAY & CHRIS SELF – SPEARFISH CREEK

A full face helmet is not a bad idea for the three sections described below. Once the creek drops into the canyon it gets steeper, very fast, often shallow water with sharp rocks below. Rolling here could be ugly without proper protection. Here are some descriptions of the 3 restored sections of Spearfish Canyon, upstream to down.

SAVOY TO LONG VALLEY CAMPGROUND.

Class II with a Class III drop and chute at the end. Best run when Spearfish Creek in town is flowing above 120 CFS, preferably at least 200 CFS.

Be very wary of downed trees and wood on this run. Much of the stream in this section can be scouted from the highway, but some areas require scouting. The large spruces in this section of canyon are prone to fall and frequently block the creek.

CHRIS SELF STRAINER INSPECTOR - JUST BELOW SAVOY

Park at Savoy and walk your kayak and gear down the nature trail to the foot bridge across the creek downstream from Spearfish Falls. In early season with high snow it's possible to slide in some of this distance. Putting in above Spearfish Falls is possible but the foot bridge below the falls is often too low to safely get under. The rapids at the footbridge are a nice set of Class I - II rapids (depending on flow). The first eddy on river right 50 yards downstream before the left bend is a good place to regroup with everyone in the party.

The majority of this run is Class II with a few drops that are a bit harder and some places where quick turns are needed. Watch for downed trees and low hanging limbs a two-foot low head dam in the middle of the run that cannot be seen from the road. At higher flows (above 200 CFS) the dam has a sticky hydraulic.

JUSTIN'S "MYSTERY MOVE" ON THE LOW HEAD DAM HYDRAULIC

On the final part of this run, the creek channel narrows and drops more quickly. This section can be scouted by walking along the highway on the first major road bend upstream from the picnic ground. A series of small drops and pools lead to a narrow fast set of rapids. The rapids are best run on the right side of the river left channel. A large boulder in the

BEN & MIKE – CAMPGROUND PLAY WAVE

middle of the rapids needs to be avoided. There isn't much of an eddy pool below the rapids before a large log strainer crossing the creek. It can be run far river right by boofing over the top of the strainer, or far river left with a sculling move to scoot underneath.

There are a few play waves at the picnic ground that are great fun. The rapids below the picnic ground are very fun to run but beware of the nasty galvanized culverts just downstream, they must be portaged around, scout and eddy river left. Time: 1.5 hours+

LONG VALLEY PICNIC GROUND TO 11TH HOUR GULCH

The paddle from Long Valley lane to the rock-fall at 11th Hour Gulch is the most sustained and exciting section of Spearfish Creek! This section of the creek is steeper and, narrower than any other part of the canyon. It includes a few places too narrow for a kayak to go through without proper flow AND excellent boat control. There are also areas where deadly rock pins are very possible. The issue of downed trees is also a continued threat. This is a perfect example of how flow levels can change a creek. Scout FIRST!

SPEARFISH CREEK – HIGH FLOW ON A SNOWY SPRING DAY

The Rapids below the Long Valley Picnic Ground are a nice, fun, steeper drop. They are bony in lower flows, but get more fun above 200 CFS. After this drop, be ready to eddy out for a mandatory portage several hundred yards downstream. Two corrugated metal culverts make up the crossing point for Long Valley Lane. This type of culvert can have nasty pieces of metal hanging around the intake that can really mess up your day. While the culvert's have been run, it is best to hop out at one of the nice eddies above the culverts and hike around them. This section below long Valley Lane down to 11th Hour Gulch was opened up spring of 2011. First descent

CHRIS – SPEARFISH CREEK

honors go to Ben and Caleb Teneyck who, in early 2008 put up with portaging around all those downed trees. Second descent (with fewer strainers) credit to: Mike, Justin, Scotty, Chris, and 2 visiting Canadians. This is classic "creeking." It should not be considered by anyone without a very high level of experience and a river rescue plan.

11TH HOUR GULCH TO MAURICE INTAKE

This section of restored Spearfish Creek is much like the upper section from Savoy to Long Valley Picnic Ground, but a bit more narrow at points. It includes several long nice Class II rapids punctuated by drops that can approach Class III or higher with larger flows.

THE TEN EYCK BOYS – JUST ABOVE MAURICE INTAKE

This part of the canyon is defined by strainers. Downed trees are extremely common and can increase the difficulty and danger here immensely. Most of the trees are cut by beavers, so new ones pop up all the time. This section MUST be carefully scouted prior to any run. Fortunately scouting from the road is fairly easy, but some of the most difficult parts of this run remain hidden from view and must be scouted by getting out of the boat and checking.

The put in is at the 11th Hour Gulch pull off. It's possible to put in above the rock-fall and paddle under the tunnel made by the rocks. However, in the spring of 2011, a new beaver-cut strainer about 200 yards below the rock fall requires careful scouting. It's easier to take the turnoff before 11th

SPEARFISH CREEK – LOW BRIDGE

Hour and put in below the strainer. The first potential hazard is a low wooden bridge. This bridge can be difficult to get under during times of high flow. At 100 CFS, it's no problem, but it gets dicey with higher flows.

The crux of this run comes after that bridge. It includes a nice narrow set of rapids that start at a cabin on river right. The rapids drop river left and out of sight. It's impossible to see this section from the road there is also no good view from the boat, so scouting on foot is mandatory. The rapids drop quickly and require some quick turning to avoid getting pinned on the large boulders on either side of the creek. Putting one boater up to spot this section with a throw rope is a good safety precaution, especially during higher flows. After this drop the rapids continue. It's not too hard to paddle eddy to eddy diligently checking for strainers along the way. Make sure everyone in your paddling group knows river signals. Stay alert and be ready to eddy out and portage at any time.

The rapids continue to wind through this gorgeous canyon with steeper drops here and there. One of the best play waves on this entire stream (and

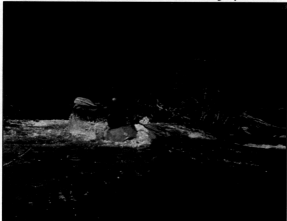

arguably among the best in the hills) is located a few hundred yards below the confluence of Squaw Creek and Spearfish Creek. (Upstream Squaw Creek flows through what's locally known as Devils Bathtub) The wave is well formed across most of the stream but the pool below the wave isn't that deep. The eddies on this wave are easy to catch when coming downstream, but may be harder to catch if you're kicked out of the wave and want to paddle back up and in. Time: 2 hours

LEROY HENDERSON CATCHES AN EDDY

MAURICE INTAKE TO THE CITY OF SPEARFISH

This normally dry section of canyon rarely receives enough water to make for good paddling. Flows have been high enough during a handful of weeks out of the last decade. It has never been run to anyone's current knowledge. It also appears to have very high number of strainers, and any paddle of this section would require extreme caution.

CHRIS, JUSTIN, MIKE, LEROY (LEFT TO RIGHT)

DRAINAGE 5 - BOXELDER CREEK

What a pleasant surprise Boxelder Creek has been! Boxelder creek is a recent discovery; the creek simply did not have water to float a boat in until 2008. There is still a huge loss of flow where Boxelder Creek flows over and into the porous limestone layer at the bottom of Doty Springs Canyon. We now paddle three paddle routes upstream of Doty Springs.

JOB CORPS TO BOXELDER FORKS

Scotty Nelson earned first descent credit for this surprisingly nice little run:

"Spring 2010, Box Elder Creek, Nemo Work Camp to Boxelder Forks Trail Head. Andrew Pavek and I put in where Nemo Road intersects Boxelder Creek near the Nemo Work camp. We slid in on the snow and right away we had to get out for two fences. Once we hit the work camp we were fence-free and had to get out once for a downed tree. Over all, this section is an incredibly pleasant section if the water is high enough. Class I and II rapids, very scenic, with a couple of easy man-made drops. If we could get the tree out, this section would be good for beginner kayakers. A better option would be to get permission and park at the work camp to avoid fences. Over all it is very enjoyable. "

Mike Ray also paddles this run regularly now (Mike grew up just downstream along Boxelder Creek). He added this narrative to Scotty's:

"The run on Upper Boxelder Creek begins at the Job Corps, and rolls through Boxelder Forks Campground and down to the Boxelder Trailhead on the Centennial Trail (about 1/2 of a mile upstream from the town of Nemo). This is pleasant intermediate run best paddled in high spring runoff when Boxelder is above 250 CFS at Nemo, but like any run in the higher elevations of the Hills it is common to find multiple strainers. The large spruce trees regularly fall across the creek and make for nasty hazards. All blind corners must be scouted.

The run begins on the northern fork of the creek and is joined by the south fork at the campground downstream from the Job Corps. Park near the Job Corps Education Center. The small gravel parking lot before the bridge into the education center is a fine place to park and gear up. It's not a bad idea to ask permission to park, and the staff at the center recommends leaving a note on one's car alerting those inside that the group is kayakers and not hoodlums trying to sneak beer into the youth inside (apparently this happens at this facility on occasion)

Walk out across the field and put in above the bridge. The creek winds through small easy class two drops, the strainers keep it interesting, so stay on your toes. Also the eddies here are somewhat tight in spots so have your eddy turns and river signals down so that the party can leapfrog easily in areas and turns that can be scouted from an eddy in the boat. At higher flows there are several small play waves in the campground area and some nice slightly bigger waves after the south fork enters on river right (it's easy to miss).

After the bridge at the campground the creek drops a bit faster, nice sustained stretches of moving Class I and II. It's very pleasant, but here also watch for strainers. They come out of nowhere and can pose serious dangers. There are also two low-head type dams here that do have a just a bit of hydraulic, play boats tend to get sucked back in (just slightly) and so ready to fight your way back up if you roll. At higher flows it never hurts to post a friend with a throw bag on any sort of potential hydraulic. There are take outs above the Boxelder Trailhead that can be used in lower flows as well. Make sure to make note of a dozen or so barbed wire fences below the take out and down creek to Nemo. These should be portaged around. **99**

Scotty put in the above route after he gained some good experience kayaking and developed solid boat skills and absorbed some safety training. Scotty also paddled Boxelder Creek from the above section to the Boulder Problem below. We include his very honest narrative of that section both as an example of how NOT to boat, and as an illustration of the "fence hell" the section presents. This section is NOT recommended for general paddling by Black Hills Paddlers due to the numerous fence/wire problems.

66 My experiences kayaking Boxelder Creek and Spring Creek over the last couple years probably illustrate how one should not learn to whitewater kayak. Luckily, the Black Hills Paddlers have taken me under their wing and I'm becoming a safer and better kayaker. I'm not too familiar with ranking rapids but I think my ratings are somewhat close. **99**

SPRING 2008, BOXELDER CREEK, STEAMBOAT ROCK

" I had bought a kayak in Fort Collins over spring break and wanted to test it out. My friend Josh Midge and I decided that kayaking down Box Elder creek at 6:00 am in morning at 36 degrees F would be a good idea. Neither of us had done any whitewater before. I showed up in a wet suit, Josh, bless his heart, thought that 3 layers of cotton would suffice. We put in at Steamboat Rock Picnic Area without scouting the section we were about to run. The section of rapids right after the picnic area was exciting Class II, but fifteen minutes in Josh flipped after getting stuck in a barbed-wire fence. He was too cold to continue or even carry his kayak but fortunately we were close to the road. I ran back to the car and picked him up. I had to pull his shirts off because his hands were too cold. To this day, I still give him beef for the fabric choice. "

SPRING 2008, LEHMAN HOUSEHOLD TO JOHNSON SIDING ROAD INTERSECTION.

" Andrew Pavek and I got permission from the Lehmans to park on their property and kayak down. The creek was pretty high, around 300 CFS, so many fences were under water. This section is super fun and relatively safe. A section about half way through there is an undercut cliff to be careful with. The best sections are where the river gets channeled between narrow sections of rocky canyon. I had bought my first kayaking helmet (instead of a bike helmet) and it came into good use. I flipped going through a channeled section and hit my head hard enough that my helmet got ripped off. Watch out for fences in the later half. Class II or III rapids for most of the section. "

SUMMER 2008, NEMO TO STEAMBOAT ROCK

EDITOR'S NOTE: This is not a recommended run! There is fun to be had in the drops here, but there are way too many fences for safety's sake

" Mike Stafford, his sister Whitney Stafford and I did this section together. The Staffords had learned to kayak at the Atlantic Mountain Ranch kayaking classes that Kelly was teaching. The first section from Nemo through the Twin Peaks Meadow was slow and tedious with fences everywhere. The water was slow enough you could duck under most. Excitement began at Twin

Peaks Ranch coming out of the meadow. The creek got steep and incredibly fun. The section of rapids right above Steamboat Rock were really wild and Mike dislocated his shoulder, luckily that is where we had planned to take out. Getting permission to start at Twin Peaks ranch would be a better option next time. **"**

BOULDER PROBLEM

Normal put-in is just past Camp Columbus at the next house upstream (earth sheltered into the cliff). This is the family home of one of the premier paddlers in the Hills. Please be respectful and ask permission. Park along the driveway and carry boats across the lawn and launch in the pond.

BOULDER PROBLEM SECTION OF BOXELDER CREEK

The first drop is homemade. It pushes you river left into some brush so be aware. The next corner at Camp Columbus is badly undercut. Keep to the inside. The creek immediately splits between two tight boulders river left or for a more open route go river right. Your choice; just remember to tuck your paddle if you choose left. There is a pin boulder just past this river left chute that requires a hard right (especially above 250 CFS.) Stay inside from here, while you navigate a veritable rock garden. There is plenty of water if you have good boat control. However, this rock garden attracts a lot of wood, so scout! Next corner squeezes you between undercut wall and house-sized boulder which looks worse than it is. The creek lets up for about ? mile, but there is a low footbridge. Run it river left or portage.

Then after a long left turn you enter a pool that exits with a squeeze to a drop into another short pool that you must immediately cut a hard left, right, left and around some big boulders. It is a ?- mile float downstream and the creek runs into two fences. Usually you can slip under the first, but the second fence must be portaged around. Take out before the fences for just the upper run. Nemo Road follows the creek closely and has a nice shoulder here.

Immediately following the second fence the creek takes a hard left past a big wall and stays sustained rock hopping and boulder splitting for almost another ? mile. This takes you through a sweeping right turn and halfway down a straightaway.

Take out at Custer Gap, the only gravel road that accesses the creek on the straightaway. We call this fun run the Boulder Problem because, like a boulder problem in climbing, this run is very technical, but not that dangerous if you watch the flows. Best at 125 - 250 CFS. It's too bony (boat abuse) much below this level and exponentially more dangerous at much higher flows. It is a solid technical run that will leave you huffing, puffing and grinning! This is a quick run, too. Time: 1 hour for upper section, +or - 1 hour for the lower. It's a short shuttle as well. It's a good way for intermediate boaters to get some creeking practice on rocks that would be very unkind to them at higher flows or in bigger rivers. We still recommend you spot key drops with boaters who might swim.

CUSTER GAP THROUGH DOTY SPRINGS

Expert boaters and high flows only! A few brave souls have paddled From Custer Gap downstream past Doty Springs to where Nemo road crosses the creek again. Mike Ray, Daryl Stisser and Patrick Fleming being the first we know of. Here's what Mike has to say about it:

❝From Custer Gap to Nemo Road Bridge nearest Doty School is a 4 to 5 hour paddle. Don't consider this run without a local paddle guide and a high level of experience!

The Madison Aquifer robs Boxelder Creek of water at a series of sinkholes just below Custer Gap. So the section from the "Boulder Problem" takeout at Custer Gap down to Doty Springs is only good during times of high flow (250-350 CFS). On a good year, these flows don't last longer than a few weeks. This section of Boxelder can go for many years without proper flow.

This lack of water in this canyon has led to a large number of small diameter trees growing right out of the creek bottom. They make for very dangerous strainers in high flow. Scout and watch for possible log jams. This section is also defined by undercut limestone walls. Again - scout and avoid being trapped by keeping on the inside of river turns in high flows. There are at least two barbed wire fences on this run below Doty Springs (new fences are possible at any time) so scout and be aware of those on this run.

The first log jam is directly below Custer Gap. You begin your descent in a nice series of small drops but the creek is often clogged by trees. Watch for the slightly undercut limestone wall on river left. Below the Nemo Road Bridge the creek runs into the canyon and there are no easy exit points until the takeout. So don't go further unless you're committed. The upper section of this run includes lots of small trees growing right out of the stream bed. They can become dangerous strainers. The first set of springs, known as Gravel Spring, is river right opposite a nice limestone wall. The first bigger drops come as the canyon gets deeper and narrower. Above Doty Springs there are nice play waves at irregular intervals. The meandering canyon requires lots of scouting as blind corners are also common.

Doty Springs itself is nestled in the bottom of cavernous limestone cliffs and a great place for a break. The springs come out of the lower cliff wall river right. It's a good idea to stop and scout ahead here and consider a portage around the barbed wire fences and strainers just downstream. A nice little portage can be found up the river left bank by following the little road through the meadow. Below Doty Springs the canyon narrows for a time. This part of the canyon is extremely gorgeous. It includes several class III drops. The class III rating isn't a result of large waves but instead some serious consequences for missing a line. Also stay aware for hazards including boulders, frequent trees, and overhung canyon walls. The lower section opens up more but continues to meander requiring scouting in-places where a safe eddy can't be spotted from the boat. The last section before Nemo road is faster moving water through a set of trees. Visibility here is limited by low branches and brush it would be very easy to happen upon a strainer here so beware. The take out at the Nemo Road Bridge is hard to miss, but beware of barbed wire below - Make sure to take out at the bridge!

The final section of Boxelder from Nemo road to Black Hawk hasn't been run in many years (if ever). It remains unknown to the local paddling community. This last unknown section would likely require even more water to attempt than the upper sections-- because Boxelder continues to lose flow to the limestone in this area. No doubt this section is full of more potentially deadly hazards. It should only be considered during high flows by a highly experienced group of paddlers. **??**

DAN CRAIN- DOING SOME STRAINER MAINTENANCE

DRAINAGE 6 - RAPID CREEK

Most paddlers feel this is the crown jewel of the Black Hills paddling experience. Rapid Creek is a fabulous place to explore. There is a full range of difficulty, from Class I to IV, so know where you are when paddling one of the ten segments we divide this creek into. Rapid Creek drains the central part of the Black Hills. There are presently three dams on Rapid Creek, all man-made. The ecology of dams is less than green in many ways, but they can be good for paddlers. In this case, the middle dam, Pactola, not only divides paddle routes, but also can be very helpful by modulating downstream flows when irrigators call for water in the dry summer months.

"OATS" SURFS A WAVE ON RAPID CREEK

There is a lot of history along the creek. The posts in the stream that you will sometimes struggle to get around are remnants of bridge timbers for a historic train that plied the tourist route along the creek from Rapid City to Mystic. The Crouch Line had the distinction of having the most bridges per mile of any train in the nation. In the late 1940s, it was flooded out for the last time and went belly up. There are numerous remnants of gold diggings along the creek, as well. As you paddle think of those '76'ers who precariously worked the cliffs and sluiced along the stream. They defied General George Custer and his soldiers, who were sent to unsuccessfully enforce the 1868 and 1874 treaties with the Prairie Tribes. Even through Rapid City, the creek carries history, as the city was named after the rapidly flowing stream.

Rapid Creek itself made history on June 9th, 1972 when a localized storm cell dumped nine to fifteen inches of rain almost directly on the Rapid Creek drainage in a ten-mile radius around Rapid City! For a short time, more water was coming through Rapid City in Rapid Creek that night than through Pierre in the Missouri River! This "500 year flood" was one of the deadliest floods in our nation's history and THE deadliest in Black Hills history. 238 people lost their lives. Since 1972, Rapid City has carefully preserved and developed a floodway through town. Since the floodway cannot be built on permanently, it has become a de-facto park, meandering eight miles along Rapid Creek through the entire community.

JOSH, CHRIS, AND LESLEY ON RAPID CREEK

The local paddle club wants to develop over a mile of Rapid Creek that flows through a popular mountain biking park into a whitewater paddle park. In addition to teaching paddle skills in a safe environment, the paddle park will enhance the local paddle experience and support a growing outdoor sports population. Their first proposal for funding was denied in 2010, but the club is organizing toward another try at different funding sources in 2012.

This is what Dan Crain, a mentor for many of us and Black Hills creek paddling pioneer had to say about Rapid Creek.

❝There will be lots of good stuff to say about Rapid Creek. It contains many runnable sections from the waterfalls downstream of Rochford all the way to the confluence of the Cheyenne River. I've explored all of the sections from the play wave at Pactola spillway to St. Patrick Street just past the fairgrounds, as well as the waterfalls upstream and a small section out in the Valley near Caputa. ❞

Life is definitely stranger than fiction. One of Black Hills Paddler's last contacts with Dan Crain before he was taken in a kayaking accident in Montana, was this email he wrote in response to a visiting paddler who wanted info on Rapid Creek.

"Shawn, there are quite a few different sections of river to do from Pactola down into town. I'll give you the beta on each.

Pactola to Placerville would be Class II- and take about 1 hour. You'll need to watch out for old bridge pylons and strainers. Placerville to Johnson Siding would be a little harder Class II, watch out for wood, metal fence posts, and a low bridge. This section would take 1-1.5 hours. Johnson siding to Thunderhead Falls road takes about 1 hour and the action picks up a little more. There are numerous low bridges. Thunderhead Falls road to Hisega is a little bit harder than the section above it. It's mostly Class II with 3 or 4 Class III drops. It takes roughly 2 hours. Hisega to Dark Canyon. Tight and techy Class III, sharp rocks and wood.

At higher flows this section contains a few class IV- drops. I don't recommend this section for beginners. It takes 2-3 hours if you bomb it or 3-6 hours if you play your way down. Dark Canyon to Canyon Lake the gradient eases a bit and the river mellows back to Class II. This section, watch out for strainers. It takes roughly 1-2 hours. Canyon Lake to Hardees is Class II with a few good deep eddy lines to play in and small waves to surf. Takes 1.5-2 hours. Hardees to Memorial Park is Class II with a couple of small waves to surf and deep eddies to throw down in. Takes about 1-1.5 hours. From Memorial Park and on out into the Valley be very careful of strainers and a few low head dams. From here on down the river becomes very trashy, tons of city trash in the creek I don't recommend it. On out in the Valley the trash is not so bad and the river becomes muddy and the character changes to snapping turtles, carp, mussels etc. etc. It makes me feel like I'm in a Louisiana swamp.

The wave at Pactola is fun I'd say that right now it's a III+ hole. The levels right now are low for most of the Creek. You can bang your way down from Pactola to Johnson Siding. Kelly Lane (in the phone book) went from Pactola to Hisega this weekend and he said it was ok. Personally I'd like to see a little more water. "

Well said! Thanks Dan!

Some of Dan's description of Rapid Creek has been modified over the last decade. We now paddle upstream of Pactola, and have more put-ins and take-outs through town. The creek below the County fairgrounds is still too junky and woody to be fun. A LOT of the trash has been cleaned up, though. Here is a little deeper beta of each section.

10 BEST PADDLE-ABLE SECTIONS ON RAPID CREEK.
From Upstream to Down:
1. Rochford Road to Canyon City
2. Canyon City to Trail 40 trailhead
3. Trail 40 trailhead to Silver City, Schoolhouse Flats or Pactola Lake
4. Pactola Lake to Placerville
5. Placerville to Johnson Siding
6. Johnson Siding to Thunderhead Falls Road
7. Thunderhead Falls Road to Hisega
8. Hisega to Rapid City
9. Rapid City to Canyon Lake
10. Canyon Lake or Meadowbrook Golf Course to:
    a. Founder's Park
    b. Central HS Tennis Courts
    c. Roosevelt Park
    d. Pennington County Fairgrounds.

1. ROCHFORD ROAD TO CANYON CITY

Put in where the Mickelson Trail meets the Rochford Road, about halfway

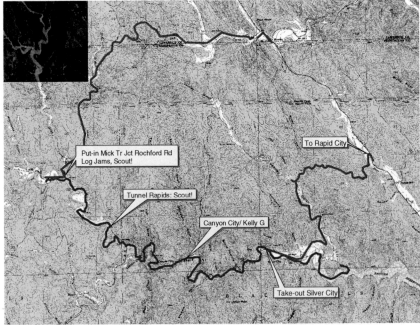

RAPID CREEK – ROCHFORD ROAD TO PACTOLA

between Highway 385 and Rochford. This part of the Hills is susceptible to lots of downed trees or strainers. They shift in number and location, so scout; carefully and often! These can be DEADLY strainers! Up here they tend to be huge logjams, not single trees. You may have to get out of your boat and portage, a LOT! (It was eleven times last time we paddled it) Flows also make a huge difference. At 100 CFS this steam is barely paddle-able. At 300 CFS you can barely get out of the way of strainers. This could be a long paddle, at least the first half until you reach a little mining town (no public access) named Mystic. Shortly before reaching Mystic, just about where the Mickelson Trail leaves the Creek there is a set of rapids that could be problematic. Scout! This is no place to get off line. The best take-out is Trail 40 trailhead way down at Silver City. This can easily become a six hour paddle with no takeout access until Canyon City which is about two-thirds of the way to Silver City. Canyon City is site of the last active mining claim along Rapid Creek. More practically, this is where the Jenny Gulch/Kelly Gulch Road dead-ends about 200 yards from the creek. This point marks a considerable easing of the difficulty.

2. CANYON CITY TO TRAIL 40 TRAILHEAD

Alternate route is to put in at Canyon City and paddle to Silver City. "If" you scout this route and it is clear of downed trees (or "wood" as paddlers say), this is actually a pretty safe section of creek. It is paddle-able down to about 80 CFS and, if treeless, we would take all but the total beginner on this route up to flows of 150 CFS. We've been in this section at 600 CFS and it gets really pushy, so stay off this section at that flow unless you are an expert paddler! Sorry, play boaters, not many play waves up here! As an alternative to driving all the way to Kelly Gulch twice, you could shoulder your boat and run to Canyon City. It's only

PAULETTE HIKES TRAIL 40

about 3.7 road miles. Paulette does this all the time!

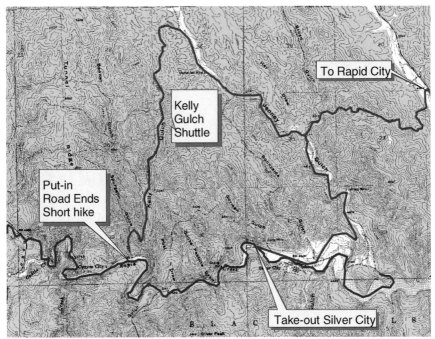

RAPID CREEK – KELLY GULCH TO SILVER CITY

3. TRAIL 40 TRAILHEAD TO SILVER CITY

At the gated road just above Silver City, begins what locals call our "lesson creek." For years, our local ACA certified instructor and area outdoors camps have gotten new boaters acclimated at nearby Pactola Lake, and then coaxed them down this pretty, short section of creek. It is also a favorite tubing run for Silver City visitors and locals. This section still has hazards, so it is imperative that you scout the whole section before putting inexperienced boaters on it. In spite of the need to occasionally remove strainers or big wood, nearly the whole section is visible from the road. If we find problem spots with new boaters we

GROUP PADDLE - TRAIL 40 TRAILHEAD

position a safety boater at each obstacle to insure success. Acceptable flows for newer boaters are 75 - 175 CFS.

Experienced boaters can run it at much higher flows (up to 450+ CFS). There are three possible take outs, depending on how much of a run you or your group wants.

TAKEOUT 1: at the junction of Nugget Gulch and Rapid Creek, just downstream from the Silver City gardens you can drive almost to the creek. Total run is just 1 river mile; 30 minutes to 1.5 hours depending on group ability.

TAKEOUT 2: another short mile downstream is a parking area we call the school house flats (you'll see why.) Pre-scout a route through the willow thicket to the parking area. It's an additional 45 minutes.

TAKEOUT 3: if you want to paddle part of the lake it is but 1.5 more miles to the Jenny Gulch picnic area. Jenny Gulch is a nice put-in or take-out

JENNY GULCH

spot nearly any time. Jenny Gulch is a no-wake zone that keeps things calm with motorboats. The lake's headwaters sport a wonderful variety of wildlife. It's an additional 1 to 1.5 hours if you take out here.

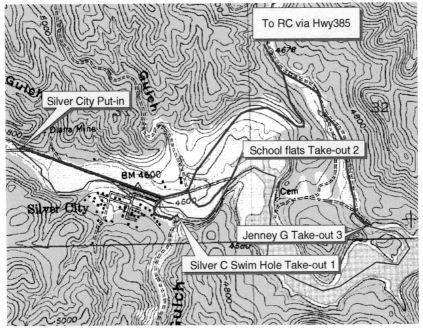

RAPID CREEK – TRAIL 40 TO PACTOLA

4. PACTOLA DAM TO PLACERVILLE

Put in at the Mickelson trailhead which is in the meadow below Pactola Dam. The gravel access road winds down the face of Pactola Dam. This paddle route takes advantage of the flats below the reservoir. The creek meanders and is just dropping into a canyon when you reach the first take-out, at the Placerville UCC Church Camp. It is a long bumpy access road from US Hwy 44 to Placerville for shuttle. The Church

PATRICK SURFS RAPID CREEK

Camp's Forest Service lease requires them to maintain public access and parking. Drive straight past the camp gate to access public parking.

This is a good beginner run, although we actually discourage using it very much because it is also a favorite stream section for Black Hills fly fishers as well. Fishermen and boaters typically get along well. However, a boat passing over a fresh rise can disrupt the fish, delaying their feeding response. The fly fishers would like this section to pursue the rise uninterrupted. If you do run it, please be considerate. Other than some sharp turns, there are a couple of places where the old bridge pilings create spontaneous, if fragile, log dams. One of these spontaneous dams, near the bottom can be problematic. Use your head and drag your boats over or around it if you are at all uncomfortable running one of these dams. There is a partial concrete dam right above the takeout that is more intimidating than dangerous. We advise you spot both. This run is best at low to moderate flows: 80 - 200 CFS. It takes 1.5+ hours.

5. PLACERVILLE TO JOHNSON SIDING

This is a favorite run for many folks. It's much like the previous run at the top, but it gets more challenging at the bottom. Put-in at Placerville Church Camp and take-out at Johnson Siding. Paddlers have permission to park in the back of church lot next to the bridge in Johnson Siding. Along the run you might have to portage one or more of those log jams against the old bridge pilings. The bottom of this run is NOT for apprehensive beginners. It's more scary than dangerous at lower flows, but here is a vexing set of bridge pilings at the McKee place that flip a lot of boats. Then, just a quarter mile downstream, behind the Johnson Siding store, the canyon closes in and it feels like enormous waves are suddenly pushing

RAPID CREEK PADDLERS

you around. Paddle through it to the take-out and you shouldn't have to swim. It takes 2+ hours.

105

6. Johnson Siding to Thunderhead Falls Road

Some folks don't like to paddle this section because they say it is like being in a fish bowl; houses line the creek all the way. Other paddlers like it because there are some nice obstacles in the creek to handle. It is a very moderate run at low flows (80 - 150 CFS), but when the flows go up (150+ CFS) big rocks in the middle of the stream get very hungry and can jam you up at several key spots. Not difficult, just don't get sucked into the rocks. Be ready to portage several potentially low bridges in this section at higher flows. There is also a smaller low head dam alongside the highway where Thunderhead Underground Falls diverts water for their tourist attraction. Take-out at the Thunderhead Falls Road bridge. Load or unload at the bridge, then park you shuttle vehicle across the highway in the Presbyterian Church parking lot. Paddlers have church permission to use the lot. Plan 2+ hours in the water.

PAULETTE SURFS RAPID CREEK

7. Thunderhead Falls Road to Hisega

This is the second most challenging run on Rapid Creek. Not for beginners, it is fun for aware, decently outfitted, intermediate paddlers. Put in at the Thunderhead Falls Road bridge off Highway 44. Paddlers have permission to park shuttle vehicles across the highway in the Presbyterian Church lot.

Trouble starts at the first turn with a rock dam mixed with bridge pilings. At most flows, this is a mandatory portage. If flows are right, and you can see a good line, boof it! Spot it if you run it! The drop is a gas to run, but it hurts both you and your boat if you twist and get crosswise or bow down in the pilings. Good potential for BOTH vertical and horizontal pins! There is also the risk of a vertical pin among the big rocks at the base of the dam.

MIKE RAY ON RAPID CREEK

The rest of the run has a good selection of challenging rocks, turns, chutes but few stoppers. Some of these go Class III in moderate flows. At this point in the creek it is time to start looking for wood strainers again, so scout! The Thunderhead Falls Road follows the creek almost all the way to Hisega so access in a pinch is pretty good.

One more often mandatory portage is opposite Thunderhead Falls parking lot. It's not visible from the road, but a big tree went down completely blocking river right. At lower flows you can pull yourself through under the trunk on the left. You must portage at higher flows (over 150 CFS) or spot the passage under the tree trunk. Just above take-out is Potter's Rapid, a primo drop with a good wave and nice safe pool at the bottom. Take-out is just downstream at the first bridge you come to. You are exiting on private property! Be sensitive. While this run can get your juices flowing and is not for beginning or even more apprehensive intermediate boaters, it pales in comparison to the next section. It takes 2+ hrs.

8. HISEGA TO RAPID CITY

If you are planning to paddle from Hisega through Dark Canyon and on into Rapid City, please consider very carefully what you are getting into. There are a number of reasons for this request. Dark Canyon is a mysterious, magnetic paddle route with several sections that are sustained Class III all the time, and one that can easily go Class IV+ depending on flows. This is a run for experienced paddlers! You need to be properly equipped, trained and have an emergency plan before running Dark Canyon. If you are going to run Dark Canyon, please, first answer these two questions. If you answer both honestly, then, whatever you decide, we have faith that you are making an "informed decision" and wish you well.

MIKE RAY ASKS: ARE YOU READY FOR THE HUMMER?

First question: Have you paddled Dark Canyon, including the "Hummer" before? If you HAVE paddled the Canyon, then I am talking to the choir. Paddle safe, laugh loud, and roar at the top of your lungs when you hit the sweet spot and slip between the walls when coming down the big chute. Read on for some more local advice.

Second question: Are you ready?

If you HAVE NOT paddled Dark Canyon before, Please seriously reconsider NOT doing it until more experienced paddlers can advise you. There are a lot of reasons:

- NO ONE should run Dark Canyon without someone in the party having experience with it.
- All paddlers coming through the Canyon need a bombproof roll, strong and off-side both!
- Don't go into the Canyon without emergency, first aid, recovery

gear, and a spare paddle. We also recommend a full face mask helmet. Even at higher flows, this is shallow creeking with sharp rocks poorly covered with water.

- It is a LONG walk out and at the least very difficult to get back to your boat if you swim and get separated from it.
- A swimmer or an empty boat can get trapped or wrapped around rocks. A yellow rental from summer 2010 stayed in the Canyon wrapped around rocks until finally washing out March 2011! The folks in the boat got themselves out, but that's all!
- Just being an expert paddler may not help. One of our best paddlers got beat up just a couple of years ago on the Hummer. He missed his line into the chute by scant feet. This pulled him into the river left rocks, where the rocks flipped him and his face hit a rock underwater. In spite of a full face mask helmet, he rolled up to stitches, broken tooth and glasses, black eyes from the helmet smashing against his head, face mask ripped off the helmet! He feels lucky, because the face guard failed while doing its job!
- A lot of us are "old" guys now, not too old to want the thrill, but too old for those kind of experiences for sure. That is also why we will likely be "old" guys for a long time. Leave ego home when paddling!

Before answering if you're ready or not, join me on a virtual trip through just one part of Dark Canyon:

The canyon darkens as you drop down past Hisega. You pause for a moment to marvel at the canyon's beauty. Other folks rarely get to experience what you are seeing, hearing, smelling, touching and will soon even be tasting. Even though you are dressed well, the water is cold and you are no as longer as fresh and excited as you were at the top. The Hummer is close and you are all tired, having been in the boats a good two hours already. You stop to rest, eat, and rehydrate. After the break, the group feels pumped and ready for some FUN and (hopefully) NOT DISASTER! But you know you have to be ready for both, because you are now approaching the "Hummer." It is easy to dismiss this random looking pile of rocks at low flows because it doesn't "look" intimidating. But this disarming jumble of rocks, which are escapees from the sheer canyon walls, sure gets hungry with about 150-250+ CFS of flow and starts rumbling.

On our virtual journey, 220 CFS of water are flowing through this "crux" move in Dark Canyon. The water pours over a set of pools with rocky banks and boat-busting rock gardens between. Forewarned is forearmed, so you stop and scout carefully. Back in your boat, the water quiets as you approach the chute and you are almost tempted into complacency. Suddenly, your horizon line disappears and you are over the top. Eight feet of vertical drop and 220 CFS of water accelerate you down a rock chute. You've already chosen a line to follow through the rocky, slippery slope: river middle, to safely slip down the chute and past the rocks threatening on the borders. If you miss your line and hit the rocks on either side, you will get flipped, or worse, pinned.

That bomber roll, cemented after hours in the pool, on-side and off-side, better not fail you if you flip. You will have to react quickly here and get right back up. There's no second chance. It just gets worse if you swim. The rocks along the creek bottom are quite sharp. They can beat you up even in your boat. But you're through! You made it!

THE HUMMER - RAPID CREEK

You give a victory holler to your spotter, standing at the ready; then eddy out and watch your buddies following. One gets flipped, misses his roll and swims. He gets to the eddy with the help of a throw-line from a spotter, and you retrieve his gear. He's shaken and a bit bruised, but thankfully okay. You want to get him home, but you all still have to get to the takeout. Everyone feels thankful they're not coordinating any of the gnarly rescues you all had planned out, just in case.

Now, open your eyes. Depending on flow, the "Hummer" is currently the only reliable Class IV rapid on this creek, but it is a long way in and just as long out. You put in at the only publicly accessible put-in for this section, at the gate upstream of Hisega Lodge. The circle drive is the only parking where you will not get towed. It is still private property, but the owner put the circle in to help. For most of the first hour, you will paddle among the houses in Hisega Canyon. Occasionally, wood can fall across the creek. Watch for it and scout; it's tough to eddy out in the middle of a drop where the bottom is blocked by a log that you missed! The run thus far is sustained Class II, some Class III.

ANDREW HENTZ IN DARK CANYON

Just above McGee Siding, you encounter two spots where the creek undercuts rocks, a quarter-mile apart. During these left-hand turns, you can get sucked into the right hand wall and pinned if you don't paddle hard away from them. These two places should be spotted with a safety boater and a rope if you have a likely swimmer with you. Next you pass the Andrew place at McGee Siding, then some big rock gardens, and finally the Falling Rock development. This all takes about two hours, and finally it's time for the Hummer. After the Hummer, it is several long, rocky miles to the take-out, which is the first public access/ parking, a small picnic area just inside Rapid City's city limits. Know that any rescue might require a long paddle. The neighbors along this part of creek value their privacy and are often NOT boater-friendly.

Are you really ready? 'Nuff said.

9. Rapid City Limits Picnic Area to Canyon Lake.

Some of the drop from Dark Canyon is still evident here, at the picnic area put-in, but it handles higher flows pretty well. About two thirds of the way to Canyon Lake (one mile into the run) you will go over a four foot rock dam. Watch out because rocks at the base of the dam fold the creek over itself and will dump the unsuspecting. There's one more fold just downstream, then a locally engineered home-made play wave, and finally some s-turns (watch for strainers) before you are in Canyon Lake. The boat ramp on your right is an easy take-out. This is not a hard section; there are just a few tricky spots. It's best at 100-200 CFS and takes 1-1.5 hours

10A & B. Canyon Lake to Pennington County Fairgrounds

10A. From Canyon Lake Dam (Parking south side of dam) you have a lot of choices. Sometimes we put-in here, below the third small low head dam

CANYON LAKE LOW HEAD DAMS AT HIGH WATER (250CFS)

(it's too shallow to be a dangerous dam, but just the right height to be a boat-beater). There is a nice wave just downstream.

10B. For a slightly (mile) shorter run put-in halfway back down Jackson Boulevard at Meadowbrook Golf Course. Below are our most common take-outs, shortest to longest distance.

Takeout A: Founder's Park
Takeout B: Central High School Tennis Courts
Takeout C: Roosevelt Park
Takeout D: Pennington County Fairgrounds

The basic run to Founder's Park is 2 plus hours. Add another hour or so for each successive take-out. Rapid City has a well-developed park system

with a bike path and greenway through the whole community along the creek. Between the bike path and the many roadside

KELLY AND TIM - LATE SEASON PADDLE ON RAPID CREEK

pullouts, there is tremendous access and many great photo opportunities.

Rapid Creek is often paddle-able all summer, thanks to irrigators downstream of Rapid City, who get their water from the upstream Pactola Dam. Rapid Creek paddlers through town benefit from this steady release of water. The creek has a tendency to undermine overgrown vegetation along the shore and suddenly drop a tree across the creek, so be aware and scout! These can be BIG trees.

ANNA, KEVIN, AND TJ ON RAPID CREEK

Rapid Creek is a fun yet very forgiving stream at low to moderate flows (80 - 200+ CFS). Above 300 CFS it is best left to experienced boaters only, as the banks get full and the creek gets pretty pushy. You don't want to swim when the creek is running high because it takes a long time to recover your

boat, and it can be very tough to get out of the current for a strainer. The biggest hazard, in general, beyond partial and full strainers, is inexperienced, underequipped boaters. It's another plug for the whitewater paddle park mentioned earlier, because it would help to safely

MIKE PROBES AN UNDERCUT BANK

train new boaters who might otherwise get in over their heads (no pun) through pure ignorance.

There are several pretty good waves for play boaters in the creek through town, although they tend to change and move a lot with varying flows. The last takeout behind the county fairgrounds office is just above a low head dam that has a nasty hydraulic at high flows.

FAIRGROUNDS HYDRAULIC – RAPID CREEK

DRAINAGE 7 – THE CHEYENNE RIVER

This filthy, fickle, grey, outrageously isolated, and breathtakingly beautiful waterway drains all of the Back Hills of South Dakota. However, the flows on many sections of the river can be hard to catch when they are high enough to paddle. On some, flows are high enough for just a weekend or two each year. Other runs are more reliable (relatively!) Be advised, though; when you DO catch the flow, it is worth the trouble!

Two "legendary" runs make this point well.

ICE HENGE

On a sunny, mid-March day a group of Black Hills Paddlers set off from the Highway 44 Bridge near Scenic. The group knew they were early in the

EARLY SEASON PADDLE ON THE CHEYENNE

season. A paddler who drives truck regularly reports on the river throughout the season. Just days earlier, Burt had called and said there was still ice on the Cheyenne at Wasta, the take-out point this day. Not wanting to be on the river during the very deadly ice break-up, paddle organizers waited till the USGS stream-flow gauges were indicating flow before setting this run.

River flows were comfortably high at about 1500 CFS. The water didn't push at all in these flows because the Cheyenne River is evolved to carry lots of water out of the Hills. The run looked to be typically beautiful for spring in Western South Dakota. The paddlers set a comfortable, but fast pace. They would spend about five hours on the water for a 25+ mile paddle. The group encountered swarms of wildlife right away: eagle, hawks, ducks, geese, etc. Shortly after the put-in, paddlers noticed great slabs of mud covered material piled above the high water line. Paddling closer to these muddy chunks of mystery stuff, the kayakers realized they were looking at monster chunks of ice! Although the river was high and fast, there was no ice in the water at all. Somehow, they had stumbled upon that magical interlude between break-up of the river's ice cover, many feet thick, and the melting that would follow this violent break-up. Giant slabs of ice were as tall as a house, larger than a semi-truck and trailer! Even the little slabs were car-sized, stacked four or five deep high on the river banks.

The goggle-eyed paddlers travelled about ten miles accompanied by this magical display of "Ice-Henge!" Eventually, this show of force began to taper off until, by the time boaters reached Wasta, there was just an occasional piece of ice on the banks, covered with insulating mud. How privileged the group felt to safely witness this fabulous example of nature's mighty nonchalance just a few short days after ice break-up!

Another run readers must know about on the Cheyenne River also involved some lucky timing:

WAVE TRAIN

This paddle trip happened in mid-July, a time when the Cheyenne River is hardly paddle-able until after its confluence with the Belle Fourche River. It had however been a very wet year, and the USGS website showed higher than normal flows. So the group of paddlers set a run from Red Shirt Table to Scenic, 32 miles downriver. On the drive from Rapid City to the put-in at Red Shirt, Justin checked USGS Waterwatch for stream flow on his smart phone (Yes, there is an App for that!). Becky actually pulled the truck over right there and conferred with Lisa and Paulette in the other shuttle vehicle. The website said flow at the put-in was just below the minimum paddlers had established to avoid excessive sand bar angst! 'Should we even try?" "Yes," was the consensus, "We're half-way there, let's go scout it at least!"

It was not a wildly enthusiastic group of paddlers who topped the hill and drove into the river valley and onto the bridge at Red Shirt Table. "What the hey?" "There's plenty of water here!" This was the first clue the group missed because the stream flow website is usually quite accurate! With their paddling zeal renewed, the paddlers unloaded, ran the hour and a half shuttle and put-in just past mid-morning.

CHEYENNE RIVER – THE DAY OF 'WAVE TRAIN'

The Cheyenne River eventually drains the entire Black Hills, with the Cheyenne River itself draining West and South slopes, while the Belle Fourche River gathers the North and East slopes, eventually to drain into the Cheyenne as well. Various creeks and tributaries drain into the river all along its course, so boaters expect flows to increase as they paddle downstream. Within a few miles, the group KNEW this was more than a little run-off! At lunch that day, about ten miles into the 32 mile paddle, there was a dawning awareness as the group looked at each other and asked, "Are you still comfortable in this water?"

The answer was still unanimous, "Yes!" In fact, that "Yes" was a very enthusiastic "Yes!" The Cheyenne River was showing her stuff. These water-rats just "happened" to be on the River, paddling a storm-surge of run-off from recent thunderstorms over the Black Hills. There was no estimating how high the river would rise with this surge, but the beautiful Cheyenne, with millions of years of experience was perfectly suited to carry widely varying amounts of water quickly downstream. Even with the speed of this storm surge, it still takes time to paddle 32 miles. Plus, the group got storm delayed when they had to take-out for an hour or so while a particularly nasty storm with lightning passed over.

Right after putting-in following the storm delay, paddlers started commenting as larger and larger wave trains formed in the fastest current. Of course each paddler "had" to take the waves head-on, and the wave trains, many three to four feet tall continued without let up till they took out near dusk at the bridge below

CHEYENNE RIVER LANDSCAPE

Scenic. Each paddler was soaking wet but not cold! (Thanks to polypro, wool, and neoprene. NO cotton!) The grey clay from the mud-saturated water crashing over their boats in the miles and miles of wave trains made each of the group look like guests at a spa in the midst of a mud pack session. Yet in spite of the great wave trains and high flow, the Cheyenne never got "pushy." Pushy is "boater speak" for water that wants to turn your boat sideways in the current, against your will. It is a sign that the streams banks are getting full. This is dangerous because as the banks fill, eddies disappear or turn to boils and whirlpools. There is no longer a nice safe eddy to take a break in. The adaptable Cheyenne River, from Red Shirt Table downstream to the Missouri River has such extensive banks that it spreads out flood water automatically and almost never gets "pushy."

The time it took to clean the truck and boats after the near dark exit from the very muddy and high flowing Cheyenne River is another story. However, en route to pick up the shuttle vehicle Justin finally got data coverage on his phone and checked the USGS Waterwatch website. You could have heard the group scream all the way back in town. The unsuspecting boaters had just paddled 32 miles in water that went from 400 CFS to 6000 CFS in the seven hours they were on it. Thank You, you beautiful, muddy, changeable River for hosting this grand adventure so graciously, and safely!

Having detailed these two legendary runs we still say that this is NOT a technical river. Avoiding strainers is easy. Swimming in it at high flow is pretty dumb as it is with any high water. Remember: feet downstream, on your back. Stay upstream of your boat if you can. Don't paddle alone! A functioning knowledge of how an eddy works or "reading the V" is helpful.

Some quicksand exists in places on the river but that is more of a threat to "4-leggeds" than "2-leggeds." The biggest hazard is running out of water. It can take hours longer than expected dragging your boat over endless sand bars to reach the rare take-out spots if you miss the flow. Sun burn, dehydration, wind and mud are more likely irritants that can spoil a trip. Cover up your exposure to the blasting sun, lock your hat on in the wind and tie shoes tight to avoid losing them forever in the mirthless muck we fondly call "Badlands gumbo." Bring water and drink it!

CHEYENNE RIVER PANORAMA

There are a few animal hazards to deal with, like rattlesnakes and bees. Just realize that you might be a number of HOURS from medical care if you get hurt, bit or stung. A good map and compass is always wise. We like to laminate pages out of the DeLorme SD Atlas and take the pages needed for the run. You shouldn't get lost, but it would be embarrassing to miss your takeout because you weren't looking for it. Adding a GPS with the route preloaded (from Google maps for example) is really handy to know where you are relative to the rest of the world. It also tracks how fast you are going and answers the occasional grating cry of, "How much farther?" Cell phones get very occasional coverage! More towers are going up all the time, so this gets better every year. Rain gear is smart as thunderstorms pop up with little warning. Canoes, rec boats to sea kayaks with a spare paddle are the recommended water-craft. ALWAYS wear your PFD!

Paddle-able parts of the Cheyenne River meander (or roar) from below Edgemont (We've heard of folks paddling above Edgemont, but have never actually met anyone making this claim) to the Missouri River. A quick top-down stream travelogue of the river includes:

PADDLING THE CHEYENNE RIVER, IN 6 SECTIONS:
1. Edgemont to Cascade Springs
2. Primal Hell, Opal or Buffalo Gap to Red Shirt Table (NOT recommended except at higher water. Lots of fences and things that go bump on your boat.)
3. Red Shirt Table to Scenic Bridge (the run of the Wave Train anecdote)
4. Scenic Bridge to Wasta (Also called IceHenge after the first boats down

that season found ten foot high, vehicle sized ice slabs thrown up on shore like an other-world graveyard.)

5. Wasta to Highway 34/73 (Four Corners) Bridge
6. Highway 34/73 Bridge to Highway 63 Bridge or Missouri River confluence

1. EDGEMONT TO CASCADE SPRINGS BRIDGE

This run is usually pretty shallow up toward Edgemont but wonderful through the Wild Horse Sanctuary the few weeks you can catch the flow. Look forward to the MAGNIFICENT canyon walls through the Wild Horse Sanctuary! Dayton Hyde, Sanctuary manager, should sell tickets for

JULIE EMERSON - CHEYENNE RIVER ABOVE RED SHIRT TABLE

this! USGS stream-flow tables are very reliable for other sections of the river, but not this one. It is best is to have a paddler friend in Hot Springs who will run down to the Cascade Springs Bridge, look at "the rock" in the river and tell you, "yeah" or "nay." Put-in below Edgemont or shorten the run up a lot by taking the Rocky Ford road off the Wild Horse Sanctuary entrance road to the river and put in at Rocky Ford about midway between Edgemont and Angostura. Take-out is Cascade Springs Bridge. Average paddle time for the shorter route 3-4 hours, nearly triple that for the whole run unless flows are really high. The good news is, shuttle for the shorter route is less than an hour. It is the shortest shuttle on the river.

2. OPAL OR BUFFALO GAP TO RED SHIRT TABLE

The Cheyenne River's personality changes quickly immediately downstream of Angostura, thanks to ridiculously low flows (Angostura rarely opens its flood gates, even in the spring as the reservoir ALWAYS seems thirsty), narrow stream bed, lots of barbed wire, electric fences and nasty strainers. Anyplace you put in below Angostura, at or past Oral, at the Buffalo Gap Bridge, or below where the river marks the Pine Ridge Reservation border, nearly all the way to Red Shirt table is questionable. The Cheyenne River through here is usually ugly, routinely impossible, yet occasionally brilliant. Primal Quest competitors in August 2009 should have renamed their 40+ miles of the Cheyenne from Oral to Red Shirt Table, "Primal Hell!"

RICK & JULIE FROLIC – CHEYENNE RIVER

Primal Quest course designer Rick paddled this section in early May at its brilliance, and warned competitors that the river would be "epic" later in the summer. By race time in August, "epic' was an understatement! Professional adventure racers took from 15 to 40 hours to push, pole and drag through here! A few (very few) of the racers actually enjoyed the in-and-out, all night, hypothermic challenge. The brilliance of May had ceded itself to the ugliness of August. If you have masochistic tendencies then for sure put in at any of the above spots. Take-out is the bridge at Red Shirt Table, whenever you get there.

3. RED SHIRT TABLE TO SCENIC BRIDGE &
4. SCENIC BRIDGE TO WASTA

These two sections, 32 & 25 river miles respectively, go from Red Shirt Table to Scenic and Scenic to Wasta. These are the two best runs on the river. Each is an easy day's paddle. Plan six or seven hours on the water for each section; more if you have to drag sand bars. Add two more hours to each end of the run for shuttle (which is short by Cheyenne River standards). The eroding banks are rich in fossils, but don't expect to see much sign of modern humans. Both sections have reasonably reliable flows

April, May and possibly into June. Check the USGS real time Water Watch stream gauges; you don't want to run either section at much less than 400 CFS if you can help it. Below Red Shirt Table this river is seldom crowded in its banks so it is seldom "pushy." There is virtually no upper limit for flow downstream from here. The river has a wide floodplain along the stream by this point and the banks can spill out onto the floodplain from here. Still, paddle carefully the few weeks each season when the water is really high.

CHEYENNE RIVER

For the Red Shirt Table run, put-in at the Red Shirt Table Bridge. Take the Spring Creek cutoff for the shuttle. Take-out 32 river miles downstream at Highway 44 Bridge below Scenic. Next run downstream, put-in at the US Hwy 44 Bridge near scenic. Parking under the bridge on the north shore is most secure unless it rains (and then you will be stuck in the mud until the "Badlands gumbo" dries.) Take the New Underwood cutoff back to I-90 or, if you are local, cut across via Sage Creek Road to the gravel Jensen Ranch Road for the shuttle. Take-out at Wasta Rest Area on I-90, 25 river miles downstream. Scout for a solid bank to take-out on well above the bridge, or live with a horrible, muddy mess as you slog through the mud at the interstate bridge! The Scenic to Wasta run is far and away the most popular paddle on the Cheyenne River, meaning a couple of dozen parties paddle it annually. The Wasta Rest Area is also the most secure place on the river to park your shuttle vehicle! *Note,* these two sections especially are prone to flash flooding from way upstream. Good for spontaneous late summer runs; bad if you are on the river camping on the sand bars. So, cook on the sandbars, but sleep up on the prairie!

5. WASTA TO HIGHWAY 34/73 (FOUR CORNERS) BRIDGE

Much of the lower Cheyenne River is as isolated as you can get nearly anywhere! A classic overnight paddle (when flows allow it) is to put in at Wasta and take out at the Four Corners/Highway 34/73 Bridges. It's 55 river miles. When driving to the take out, go east of Wasta to Philip, then straight north on Highway 73 to the bridge. It's a two-plus hour drive each way from Rapid City. Before you head out on this run, make sure flows in the Cheyenne from Wasta to its confluence with the Belle Fourche River are high enough (300-400+ CFS). Otherwise, you could drag for hours until the two rivers join. Once the two rivers join, flows are high enough almost year-round (until ice-up at least.) The real problem is public access to the confluence area. To paddle to this beautiful, isolated confluence in mid to late season water, the Belle Fourche River is often more reliable than

CHEYENNE RIVER

the Cheyenne for flows. You can usually slide along the sand bars from Hereford or Elm Springs bridges on the Belle Fourche River to its confluence with the Cheyenne and on from there with no problem

Camping is pretty much "plop where you stop." It is always best to plan ahead and get land-owner permission, but most ranchers down here tolerate campers along the river. By and large we have been responsible squatters, and there just aren't many of us yet! Avoid fires at all or limit them to sandbars in the river bed, but do NOT sleep in the riverbed! Secure your boats and bed down above the high-water line! This river is very prone to flash flooding!

We recommend overnight trips on this and the next section even at high flows because it makes for a very long recovery for an old paddler when you press hard to put 50 miles behind you in a day. Exception might be in very high water (3000 CFS+.) This is still a long day, but a real cruise. The river has a wide enough flood plain that the water can spread out and very seldom gets pushy. Another reason to camp overnight: shuttle distances on this isolated river border are outrageous; average is half the day on the lower river! Leaving a car along the Haakon, Zieback County border is risky in itself. You can usually get enough occasional cell phone coverage to call for pickup by a sympathetic, non-paddling spouse or friend when you are partway downriver and can give a better ETA.

6. Hwy 34/73 Bridge to Hwy 63 Bridge

From the Highway 34/73 Bridge you can paddle 50+ more miles downstream to the Highway 63 Bridge (again, recommended overnight.) The river with any current ends roughly at the Highway 63 Bridge. Drive through Midland, North on Highway 63 past the Highways 14/34/63 junction on the way to Pierre to the Highway 63 bridge for the take-out. This is also two-plus hours each way from Rapid City.

For a real treat, since the shuttle drive takes you through Midland, stop in the heart of downtown Midland at the Midland hotel for a good soak in the mineral baths. Something like $5.00 and they provide the towel! Then slip across the street to the supper club for a meal and a cold one. Refreshing!

Beyond the Highway 63 Bridge you are in the Missouri/Cheyenne blended water. If you do travel beyond the Highway 63 Bridge, beware extreme open water conditions on this part of the Missouri River. Plan your take-out accordingly from a Missouri River entry point. We recommend Foster Bay straight across the Missouri from the Cheyenne. It's a really long shuttle, though. Check the map first!

THE CHEYENNE RIVER

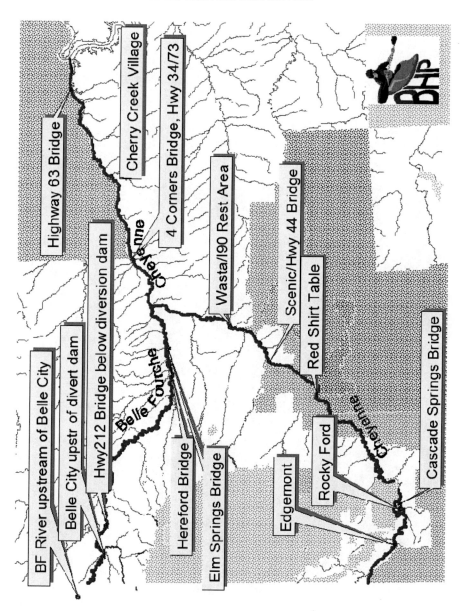

8 – OTHER RUNS

There are a handful of runs out of the Black Hills that have been paddled, yet normally are not. We list them and their current status below, but only for your information.

WHITEWOOD CREEK

Expert boater, friend, and mentor, Dan Crain had this to say in introducing Whitewood Creek to some of his expert, Class V+ boater friends

66 Whitewood Creek is a great little steep creek run in the Black Hills. It only runs on average 5-7 days in mid to late April. If you're lucky enough to catch it flowing you're in for a real surprise for the area. 99

JAKE ANDERSON – WHITEWOOD CREEK

Dan, Todd and friends bagged the first descent of this creek around spring 2000. It has scared the testosterone out of everybody with any sense who has paddled it since. Sometimes it takes a few years, but few boaters ever repeat the run after thinking about it. It's a good thing, it only runs a few secretive days a year. Definite Class IV-V with portages, big wood, and small culvert bridges at the bottom. Expert only, dry suits required. No map or directions included. Not a recommended run, but then only a few of us have ever paddled it ourselves. Some of us have scouted it and keep deciding to not run it.

ELK CREEK

This normally very quiet stream meanders all the way to the Cheyenne River. It is a classic Black Hills stream because it flows high just days or possibly a few weeks a year, sending all its water directly out of the Hills to recharge the underground aquifer. We list it here again because USGS monitors its flows, but also because paddling it has been attempted, although only part of the creek has been paddled successfully to the best of our knowledge. Spring 2009 local paddlers got calls from 2 rec boaters who had to leave their boats in Elk Creek Canyon and climb out on foot. They wanted advice on recovering their boats. Sorry, guys! Pray for rain or bring lots of rope. Either way, kiss those boats goodbye. BTW: it is illegal to just leave them there.

In the spring of 2011, Mike Ray, Patrick Fleming, Scotty Nelson, and Justin Herreman bagged a first decent of upper Elk Creek. Mike says:

❝The short stretch of Elk Creek that runs along Vanocker Canyon Road is on rare occasion high enough to paddle. Its first known descent in the spring of 2011 was made when the creek showed over 900 CFS at the USGS Gauge outside of Rapid City. One can put in on the gravel road where the creek meets the Vanocker Canyon Road for the first time. The take-out is a mile and a half down Vanocker Canyon Road at the place where the creek disappears into the canyon. It's a fairly easy, but bony stretch of creek. The section along the highway is mellow and fun, picking your way through the small trees that have grown out of the creek bed. After this the stream drops out of sight of the road around a long meander. This section is wilder and requires a bit of scouting, and the ability to make quick, tight maneuvers and accurate eddy turns. Keep an eye out for strainers here as well. The creek follows the meander around and meets the road again - the car pull off is about 100 yards downstream. ❞

MORE ON ELK CREEK

Elk Creek through the canyon below Bethlehem Cave has been scouted from the canyon rim in a few areas. It should be possible to hike down the trailhead on Runkle Road and paddle downstream until the creek meets Bethlehem Road just west of I-90. To the best of our knowledge this stretch hasn't been done. It appears that this is a fairly stout run that's got some Class IV or V spots depending on the flow and how many strainers you must avoid. This run should not be tried by any group without a high amount of experience, emergency training, rescue gear, protective gear, and a solid twelve hours to kill. It's a lovely, but a long and narrow stretch of canyon. Hiking it in the fall might be the best way to scout it.

ROCHFORD FALLS

This is a short, three-step drop just upstream of the Mystic Road turnoff off the Rochford Road. You can easily find the rapids right beside the

road. It is part of Castle Creek before it joins Rapid Creek. First Descent was again around 2000, by Dan, Todd and friends. Recent high flows are making it paddle-able again, sometimes even beyond the spring runoff. While likely Class III or IV depending on flows, this is a tricky set of drops: three narrow drops stacked tight, with virtually no pools below for recovery. Definitely spot it if you run it. This is for expert boaters only.

PACTOLA LAKE OUTFLOW/ SPILLWAY

This is the closest thing you can come to reliable "big" water in the Black Hills. Other streams like Rapid Creek through Dark Canyon and Boxelder Creek can get big as well, but this one always flows and feels big, sometimes too much so! Although the lake's outflow has been paddled a lot in the past, there is now a question of legal access, so we slipped

128

this note in back here. Remember, you are surfing in a concrete box, with NO eddy so you have to paddle like heck just to get in the wave. With no eddy, you don't want to swim either. Strongly recommend you post a spotter with a throw line. We'll leave it at that, without specifics, because of access. We believe first descent on this wave goes to Todd Andrew in 1998.

BATTLE CREEK

In spite of the fact that Battle Creek flooded badly in 1972 and again this past spring, it Is not considered paddle-able. It is fairly unique in that it has a 40-foot waterfall and year round pool in a canyon called "Hippie Hole" just a few miles below the town of Keystone. Even more unique, Dan Crain ran the waterfall around 1998. With higher than normal flows these summers, we suspect more will try. Prepare carefully, if you must. Paddle safe!

SPRING CREEK

Paulette Kirby has explored Spring Creek from Mitchell Lake to Sheridan Lake extensively. This 4 mile section has significant rock blockages and strainers but in between obstacles is a very nice paddle. Likely when the run gets described we will include a section on Spring Creek. Spring Creek then flows into and out of Sheridan Lake, one of the larger lakes actually within the Black Hills.

While the creek is big enough that it "should" be paddle-able, downstream of the lake the outflow valve on Sheridan Lake has been broken for many years. Typically, the creek downstream of the dam would dry up completely by July every year. Finally, the valve is repaired and we have big runoff! So, other than a few local boys who tried and destroyed canoes on the creek years ago, Scotty Nelson gets first descent credit summer of 2010, in quite high flows.

Be forewarned this creek has serious access issues! It drops into a canyon below Sheridan Lake on USFS land, reemerges back along the highway for just a few miles, then drops into another canyon where the land turns private. It stays that way all the way to the edge of the Black Hills. The upper section of this creek has potential to be a nice run if we can get an access plan together. The middle section has no public access. The bottom section below where Scotty took out (at Storm Mountain Camp) is jumbled with huge rocks, log jams and the creek flows through the limestone layer encircling the Black Hills. In this case flooding over eons has carved deadly, boater devouring underwater caves in the limestone as it flows past the Stratobowl. Black Hills Paddler Kelly was one of those local boys "trying" to paddle Spring Creek in a canoe so many years ago, but has hardly looked at the creek since. Scotty has this to say about his run:

❝ Spring 2010, Spring Creek, Spring Creek Trail Head to last Spring

---

EDITOR'S NOTE: Again, this run is included because it now "has" been paddled. Ideal flows are still unknown. It still is not considered a recommended paddle route. Downstream of Storm Mountain Camp is not considered paddle-able due to lots of wood, entrapment caves, and poor access

---

Creek intersection on Sheridan Lake Road Andrew Pavek and I noticed that Spring Creek looked kayak able. I don't know the actual flow rate and I don't know if the flow rate online is accurate. At first there were a few fences but that was not a big deal. Later on there were some really fun rapids. Class II and a couple Class III-ish rapids. This is a fun intermediate section of creek.

Spring Creek intersection on Sheridan Lake Road to Storm Mountain. Andrew Pavek and I did this the next day and it was wild! By this time, Andrew and I had learned that eddying out and scouting ahead are important. Class III and possibly even Class IV rapids exist and everything is really exciting. Make sure to scout ahead everything because there are some dangerous spots with no easy way to hike out. Pull out at Storm Mountain. There are a couple of low bridges to look out for right before you pull out. We called ahead and Storm Mountain was cool with us parking there. You have to hike up about a half a mile with your kayak up to the parking lot. We didn't flip ever but in 20/20 hindsight, we probably should have been better at rolling before doing this section. After doing this section we were motivated to practice rolling, because if we were to flip we would probably be S.O.L. Also I need to get a throw bag, first aid kit and knife. Overall this section is the wildest kayaking that I have done. ❞

FRENCH CREEK

We have heard of people paddling canoes on the lower section of French Creek Primitive Area long ago, but most of us grew up and concentrated our paddling in the Northern Hills. There hasn't been water in the southern

Black Hills for this creek to run well in over a decade. Now we are cycling into more snowpack and spring rain, so in spite of a good bit of the creek having wilderness designation and no organized access, someone will likely bag this very erratic creek soon. Recent scouting found a major log jam below Fisherman's Point and above French Creek Narrows. It is included on this list mainly because there is a gauging station at the upper end of it near Custer, so we can watch the flows while paddlers wait for enough water to run it.

FALL RIVER

Fall River Falls "could" be a nice short technical set of drops, but a tragic series of swimmer fatalities years ago caused the County to pass an ordinance forbidding ANY recreational use of the Falls. The rest of Fall River is hot springs fed and not worth paddling because of legal misunderstanding, frequent very low bridges, poor access, and so much corrosive chemical in the warm water. Dissolved calcium coats and corrodes everything it gets on. First descent: We know of at least one local youth, Brett Hart, who paddled Fall River through town about 1980. Still, we assume he was not the first. First of our current paddle group was Justin Herreman in 2000. He says "never again, scraped knuckles and too much boat abuse."

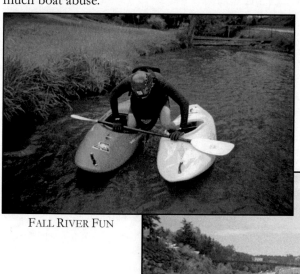

FALL RIVER FUN

Ten Items of Vital, Basic Paddling Gear

Items 1-5 are the American Canoe Association's 5 Essentials. These are the must have items that are necessary for all levels of whitewater paddling.

1 - Kayak, Canoe or Boat

Know your boat. There are many options for varying experience levels and paddling styles. A "safe" boat for one paddler may not be as safe for a less experienced partner. Example: A "rec" boat will not turn out of the current as easily as a whitewater boat, but its keel will make it go the direction you point it better. It is also very difficult to Eskimo roll a wider recreational boat back up when you flip.

2 – Paddle

Yes, this is safety gear. A good quality, properly fit paddle makes each stroke more effective and less tiring, thus safer. Learn the difference between offset or straight paddle blades then make up your own mind as to which you prefer. Typically, flat water paddles are longer than whitewater paddles. The shorter whitewater paddle will make a huge difference in your paddle stroke on shallow, narrow creeks. The longer flat water paddle will allow you to paddle at a lower angle, more efficient stroke and lower wind resistance when cruising out on a lake. Don't scrimp here. A quality paddle will make a HUGE difference in your day!

3 - Personal Flotation Device (PFD) or Life Jacket

This piece of safety gear is a necessity that must be worn whenever you are on the water. Wear your PFD whenever you paddle any stream or lake! This goes even for those boaters that are expert swimmers. Cold, fast water can easily render you unable to keep yourself above water. A securely fitted PFD (Coast Guard Type III or better) will keep you upright and afloat. Always fasten and adjust your PFD before you enter your boat. It may be legal, but NEVER store your PFD in the boat and wait till you capsize to put it on. Again, quality counts in fit and comfort as well. Your life depends on it!

4 - Helmet

While arguably not necessary on a large lake, your helmet is an essential piece of safety gear in moving water. Rivers and creeks have rocks and boulders, often submerged just below the surface where they are hard to see. In the event you flip your boat, whether you roll up or wet exit, a good helmet will protect your head from injury. Think about adding a face mask to your helmet if you do a lot of creeking. Don't thump your melon. Get a GOOD helmet that fits, and WEAR IT!

5 - Spray Skirt

The spray skirt keeps water or spray from flooding over the gunwales or cockpit rim of your boat and swamping it. Make sure you know how to safely wet exit your boat before attempting to paddle any water. A well-practiced Eskimo roll combined with a properly fitted spray skirt can save you a very cold swim. A skirt will also keep you safer in waves on the lake or stream and prevent you from having to bail out your swamped boat even if you don't flip.

6 - Flotation

This is another essential piece of safety gear. Serious whitewater boaters and sea kayakers have long known of the safety provided by float bags during boat recovery in big water. Remember, water weighs eight pounds per gallons. With the average recreational kayak capable of holding 80-90 gallons, your boat can go from a svelte 40 pounds to over 700 pounds when full of water! Float bags take the place of much of that water. This displacement keeps your boat floating higher in the water, making your kayak or canoe much more manageable to recover if you do flip or swamp your boat and have to swim.

7 - Proper Clothing

Make sure that you are properly dressed for immersion. Cotton jeans and t-shirt are not safe apparel to wear on the lake or down the creek when water temps in the Black Hills are 33-55 degrees year-round. Synthetic clothing wicks moisture from your skin and helps you avoid hypothermia. Dry suits and wet suits are excellent options in early season, cold water conditions. Paddle Jackets help in less severe conditions. Most of us wear at least a paddle jacket at all times in the creeks and usually on lakes as well. Don't forget your head and hands! Seventy-five percent of your body's heat is lost through your head. A neoprene beanie under your helmet or a good stocking cap will conserve a lot of body heat, keeping you much warmer. Stiff fingers don't work well with a paddle, either. Neoprene gloves or mittens help keep fingers flexible. Packing a set of warm clothes along with you in a dry bag (which then doubles as one of your float bags) is always a wise idea. A second set of warm clothes at the takeout will keep you from shivering too much while loading up for the drive home. Footwear of some type is also important. The rocks in our local creeks and lakeshores can be very sharp. If your feet are numb you might step on a sharp edge and split your foot open without even realizing it. Make sure your choice of footwear fits inside your boat while on your feet!

8 - RESCUE GEAR

Rescue rope throw bags, tow lines, Rescue PFD, rescue knife, pin kit, paddle floats, bailing pumps are all good items to have. If you don't know how to use them, don't carry them. If you can safely use them, each paddler should carry what they are comfortable with. Remember to practice using them so you are ready when you NEED them.

9 - COMMON SENSE & GOOD JUDGMENT

This is the most important piece of safety gear you own, many say more important than your PFD. Good judgment and experience are what keep you safe and alive. If something makes you uncomfortable or doesn't feel safe then don't do it! It is better to walk a rapid safely and paddle it another day when the water is lower or safer. Paddle across that wide lake when the sky isn't so threatening. Knowing your skill level, comfort zone and what you can safely and comfortably paddle will help keep you safe, warm and happy.

10 - LESSONS

Lessons from a qualified instructor are a great idea to help you paddle safely regardless of whether you intend to paddle lakes or streams. Contact Chad Andrew, an ACA certified instructor who offers multiple classes year-round. Chad's email address is powerof3@q.com. He offers a wide range of classes for all skill levels. Chad will also customize a class for your family, group or event. He has special-use permits for all of Rapid Creek drainage. Have Chad design a class around your favorite run!

TODD ANDREW SURFS A WAVE IN COLORADO

INTERNATIONAL SCALE OF RIVER DIFFICULTY

This is the American version of a rating system used to compare river difficulty throughout the world. This system is not exact; rivers do not always fit easily into one category, and regional or individual interpretations may cause misunderstandings. It is no substitute for a guidebook or accurate first-hand descriptions of a run.

Paddlers attempting difficult runs in an unfamiliar area should act cautiously until they get a feel for the way the scale is interpreted locally. River difficulty may change each year due to fluctuations in water level, downed trees, recent floods, geological disturbances, or bad weather. Stay alert for unexpected problems!

As river difficulty increases, the danger to swimming paddlers becomes more severe. As rapids become longer and more continuous, the challenge increases. There is a difference between running an occasional class-IV rapid and dealing with an entire river of this category. Allow an extra margin of safety between skills and river ratings when the water is cold or if the river itself is remote and inaccessible. The six difficulty classes:

CLASS I RAPIDS
Fast moving water with riffles and small waves. Few obstructions, all obvious and easily missed with little training. Risk to swimmers is slight; self-rescue is easy.

CLASS II RAPIDS: NOVICE
Straightforward rapids with wide, clear channels which are evident without scouting. Occasional maneuvering may be required, but rocks and medium-sized waves are easily missed by trained paddlers. Swimmers are seldom injured and group assistance, while helpful, is seldom needed. Rapids that are at the upper end of this difficulty range are designated "Class II+".

CLASS III: INTERMEDIATE
Rapids with moderate, irregular waves which may be difficult to avoid and which can swamp an open canoe. Complex maneuvers in fast current and good boat control in tight passages or around ledges are often required; large waves or strainers may be present but are easily avoided. Strong eddies and powerful current effects can be found, particularly on large-volume rivers. scouting is advisable for inexperienced parties. Injuries while swimming are rare; self-rescue is usually easy but group assistance may be required to avoid long swims. Rapids that are at the lower or upper end of

this difficulty range are designated "Class III-" or "Class III+" respectively.

CLASS IV: ADVANCED

Intense, powerful but predictable rapids requiring precise boat handling in turbulent water. Depending on the character of the river, it may feature large, unavoidable waves and holes or constricted passages demanding fast maneuvers under pressure. A fast, reliable eddy turn may be needed to initiate maneuvers, scout rapids, or rest. Rapids may require "must" moves above dangerous hazards. Scouting may be necessary the first time down. Risk of injury to swimmers is moderate to high, and water conditions may make self-rescue difficult. Group assistance for rescue is often essential but requires practiced skills. A strong eskimo roll is highly recommended. Rapids that are at the lower or upper end of this difficulty range are designated "Class IV-" or "Class IV+" respectively.

CLASS 5: EXPERT

Extremely long, obstructed, or very violent rapids which expose a paddler to added risk. Drops may contain** large, unavoidable waves and holes or steep, congested chutes with complex, demanding routes. Rapids may continue for long distances between pools, demanding a high level of fitness. What eddies exist may be small, turbulent, or difficult to reach. At the high end of the scale, several of these factors may be combined. Scouting is recommended but may be difficult. Swims are dangerous, and rescue is often difficult even for experts. A very reliable eskimo roll, proper equipment, extensive experience, and practiced rescue skills are essential. Because of the large range of difficulty that exists beyond Class IV, Class 5 is an open-ended, multiple-level scale designated by class 5.0, 5.1, 5.2, etc... each of these levels is an order of magnitude more difficult than the last. Example: increasing difficulty from Class 5.0 to Class 5.1 is a similar order of magnitude as increasing from Class IV to Class 5.0.

CLASS VI: EXTREME AND EXPLORATORY RAPIDS

These runs have almost never been attempted and often exemplify the extremes of difficulty, unpredictability and danger. The consequences of errors are very severe and rescue may be impossible. For teams of experts only, at favorable water levels, after close personal inspection and taking all precautions. After a Class VI rapids has been run many times, its rating may be changed to an appropriate Class 5.x rating.

Reprinted with permission from American Whitewater

First Aid on the Water

A small. waterproof first aid kit is always smart to have in your boat. While how small and basic is your choice, no boater first aid kit is usable if it isn't waterproof! This is where we as paddle boaters depart from the rest of the outdoors community, because water repellent or water resistant is not waterproof! Black Hills Paddler Justin's first aid kit (that several other paddlers have copied) is in a small dry bag stored inside a big mouth Nalgene bottle with spare glasses, headlamp, multi-tool, a trash bag, small sunscreen, bug dope, a fire source, two energy bars, and some top quality duct tape. If he can remember, he will slip his cell phone in the Nalgene and screw the top on tight.

Remember when making up your kit, a Black Hills boater's first aid kit is not intended to help at a car wreck. It is either to comfort an "owie" on the water or get to a spot for the life-flight helicopter to land. The Black Hills are rural and rough, but we are not remote or particularly wild. Cell phone coverage continues to improve every year, which puts emergency help even closer. Most of the time, paddlers are but a few hours from professional medical help.

Here's what we carry and why. We have used all of the above items over the years, although sometimes for unexpected, almost comical reasons:

1 - DRY SKIN CLOSURES / STERI-STRIPS: These stick like band aids only dream of. They are however, worthless with any moisture at all on the skin!

2 – SUPERGLUE: This is absolutely the best way to close a wound in a damp environment. Clean the wound with the alcohol pads in your first aid kit and glue that deep cut right up. Next stop the emergency room, but at least the bleeding stopped!

3 - LATEX GLOVES: These keep you safe from bodily fluids. They are also helpful with other icky clean-up. You will be glad they are there when you have to clean up doggy-doo that you squished through your fingers while pushing your boat into the water! Ick!

4 -TOILET PAPER: When you got to go, you got to go. Please don't litter! Pack it out or go without!

5 – FORCEPS: Extremely handy when you need to pull cactus spines from a buddy's 'tush after a lunch stop along the Cheyenne River.

6- MEDICATION: Plan for longer than the expected paddle time. What would you need if stuck outside for 24 hours?

7 - SPACE BLANKET: Most of us have never slept in one, but we've huddled under them when wet and cold.

8- GLASSES: Many of us are getting to where we can't see much without them. What if your regulars were at the bottom of a lake or creek and your spares were at home? Sunglasses save immeasurable wear and tear on your eyes from sunlight reflected off the water.

9 – HEADLAMP: Something has already gone wrong for you to be out on the water after dark, but it is handy for packing up and getting home. If you intend to be out after dark, a light source is necessary for navigation.

10 – MULTI-TOOL: This repairs your boat, cuts a branch to clear a jam, removes a fish hook, pulls a splinter… The uses are endless.

11 - TRASH BAG: Yes, it is a good place for garbage, but it also makes an emergency rain coat. Use it as a dry place to sit on a muddy Cheyenne River bank. You use it to store filthy Badlands gumbo-caked gear in during the drive home.

12 – SUNSCREEN: If you are fair skinned, getting fried gets serious fast! Even a good hat won't prevent a burn from sun reflecting off the water's surface!

13 - BUG DOPE: After being "bugged" and experiencing the wall of skeeters descend at sunset, no one can cover up enough. DEET is hard on skin and gear, but it works very well!

14 - DUCT TAPE: This is a toolbox on a roll. Use it for an emergency splint, hold a wet bandage in place, patch a hole in your boat or splice a broken paddle shaft. Wrap three-plus feet of fabric quality duct tape around the center of your paddle shaft or around the bottom of your water bottle.

The loaded Nalgene bottle weighs under two pounds, is waterproof, and all first aid gear because when things first go wrong on a paddle, it gives you more options to aid yourself. Take what you feel you need from this. Just think about it first, before you are on a paddle route. Oh, yeah; tie or clip this kit securely in your boat, please. Give yourself a break so when things don't go right, you've got a head start!

PADDLE SIGNALS

Paddle signals are too-seldom taught, and way too frequently ignored. To paddle safely on a lake or stream, with experienced or novice paddlers, you WILL need to keep in touch. A shout just won't cut it on a loud rapid or when spread way out on a lake when, for example, a slow paddler needs help. Fortunately there is a universal set of paddle signals that EVERY paddler should become familiar with. You can also make all of these signals without a paddle. Just wave your arms in the same exaggerated motion.

1 - ARE YOU OK? Pat yourself on the head in an exaggerated motion. If the intended paddler IS OK, answer the same way. If not, then do nothing and someone should come running!

2 – CONTINUE: Paddle held straight up, tall and still. Example: you want to go over a drop where you cannot see the paddler in front of you any longer. Front paddler holds paddle straight up to tell you it is clear for you to go.

3 - RIVER RIGHT OR RIVER LEFT: Hold your paddle up and point at angle toward the river side that paddlers behind you should go. Don't confuse yourself with right and left. Just go the direction the paddle is pointing. The paddle always points to safety!

4 – DANGER: Don't come this way! Get out of the current and wait! Paddle held straight up and swung in a wide circle repeatedly. For example, use this if someone dumped on a blind drop and you need to wait for the run to clear.

5 - STOP! Hold paddle overhead horizontally with both hands. Example: Group is getting too spread out and rear paddler signals paddlers ahead to hold up and wait.

Whether you are on a lake or river, creek or pond, are tired or wet, encounter lightning, wind or suddenly see rapids or a strainer, paddle signals WILL help your entire group. Please learn them and review them before each trip!

Boat Wash Program

Please help fight the spread of exotic and invasive species. As said before in the etiquette section: We don't live in a bubble here in the Black Hills. As boaters who paddle our boats on lots of different streams and lakes, we have a responsibility to help control the spread of a whole raft of invasive species. The Black Hills surface water is already infested with a number of invasive species that thrive because the normal biological controls for them are missing.

This happens when the organism is introduced to waters outside of its home range. Let's do our part to keep these invaders at bay. Boat racks and gear closets in our garages are now beginning to sport garden sprayers containing a 10% Clorox solution. The number of invasive species already in our remote Black Hills amazes us. Lots of other places have invasions that are so much worse. Please help us prevent and limit the spread of these species. Here is a Black Hills update, current as of Spring, 2011:

1 - DIDYMOSPHENIA GEMINATA "DIDYMO" THE Black Hills is the ONLY place for a long way where Didymo blooms like this! This is the stuff that looks like decomposing baby diapers. It gets so thick in our favorite creek that you can just scoop up handfuls at a time. There is quite a story behind researching solutions to Didymo. Ask a local paddler or fly-fisher! It is known to be in Rapid Creek and Castle Creek.

2 - CURLY LEAF PONDWEED: Found in several water bodies across the state, including Sheridan Lake, Canyon Lake, Rapid Creek and Angostura Reservoir.

3 - EUROPEAN RUDD: Populations of this invasive fish commonly used as bait are scattered throughout the state, found in Black Hills Lakes: Pactola, Sheridan and Angostura.

4 - COMMON CARP: The common carp is native to Asia which has been introduced to every part of the world with the exception of the Middle East and the poles. This fish is on the List of the world's 100 worst invasive species and can be found in most waters throughout the state.

5 - OPOSSUM SHRIMP (Mysis relicta): These tiny crustaceans have been found in Pactola Reservoir.

6 - RED-RIMMED MELANIA (Melanoides tuberculata): This common aquarium species of snail was released into Cascade Springs and now thrives along Cascade Creek in Fall River County as a result of the year-

round warm water temperatures provided by thermal hot springs.

7 - TAMARISK "SALT CEDAR": This invasive tree has been reported in several Black Hills counties including: Butte, Custer, Fall River, Meade, and Pennington.

8 - PURPLE LOOSESTRIFE: The presence of this flowering plant has been established in several areas statewide, including: Rapid Creek (Pennington County) and Orman Dam (Butte County.)

The Boat Wash Cooperative Program recommends that all boaters:

- Always Inspect Equipment - Look for visible plants and animals before traveling.
- Remove everything from equipment.
- Always Drain Water - Eliminate water from equipment before transporting.
- Always Clean Equipment -Wash equipment with 140-degree water (your local car wash hot water rinse), 10% chlorine bleach and water solution, or a hot saltwater solution. Don't forget to wash clothing after wading or swimming in infested waters.
- Always allow equipment to dry for 5 days (if possible) before entering new waters.
- Always Report Questionable Species because early detection may help prevent spreading.

You can help keep aquatic nuisance species out of South Dakota waters!

TRITE BUT TRUE: GIVE A HOOT DON'T POLLUTE!

ENTRANCE FEES AND USER FEES

This may get a bit confusing. Please refer to individual lake descriptions for specifics. The seven different government agencies create a widely varied management picture for Black Hills lakes.

The Black Hills National Forest (BHNF) does not charge an entrance fee for lakes it manages. Instead, they charge a day use fee of $4.00-$6.00, per vehicle, per day. South Dakota Game, Fish and Parks (SDGFP) does not charge day use fees. The Parks do charge entrance fees from $4.00 to $14.00 per vehicle per day or week. The US Army Corp of Engineers built and manages two paddle-able lakes near Hot Springs (Cottonwood Springs and Cold Brook) and charges no entrance or user fees. The Bureau of Reclamation operates two large dams outside the Black Hills, the Angostura Reservoir and the Belle Fourche Reservoir. Both are managed for recreation use by the SDGFP, so SDGFP entrance fees apply. Most of the managed area around the Belle Fourche Reservoir is also a National Wildlife Refuge, which is controlled by the United States Fish and Wildlife Service. Recreation is managed by SDGFP for just $4.00 per day. There is also a National Wildlife Refuge incorporating the much smaller, no services, Bear Butte Lake where SDGFP recreation management charges a $8.00 per day entrance fee. Just a couple of miles from Bear Butte Lake lies a small Bureau of Land Management-owned reservoir with no fees or services. Adding to the confusion, depending on the park, SDGFP charges entrance fees year-round, while BHNF only charges daily recreational user fees during the summer season.

Camping fees vary widely as well, varying from $7.00 to $31.00 per night for a tent site. Campsites at the more popular lakes must be reserved through a central reservation system, although most campgrounds retain a few "same day reservation" campsites. Camping fees are separate from entrance or day user fees.

You are welcome to try and sort these fees out on your own, but we recommend just bringing a lot of small bills, because most fee sites depend on you self-paying with the correct fee at the pay station in the parking lot. Or, simply buy an annual pass from the two fee agencies. A Black Hills National Forest annual recreational users pass is $20.00 Standard or $30.00 Premium. Premium adds access to Pactola and Sheridan Lakes. Annual entrance pass for South Dakota State Parks is $28.00, second vehicle $14.00. These will cover all your paddle needs, with no hassle. Otherwise it is $4.00-$14.00/day or week in state managed parks, $4.00-$6.00/day to park at national forest lakes. Go with the annual passes! They are available in person at park or forest offices, on site, by mail or online.

Licensing Your Longer Lake Boat

If you thought entrance and user fees were confusing, read on:

Beware! If your boat is over twelve feet in length, you must license it in South Dakota. If you and your boat are from out of state, you must be legal in your home state to be legal in South Dakota, unless you live out of state and keep your boat in South Dakota for more than 60 days in a single year. Then it must be registered according to South Dakota law. Non-motorized canoes and kayaks are not titled. However, all watercraft over 12 feet must be registered and licensed.

If you want to take a boat that does not require licensing into a state that DOES require licensing for that boat, you MUST comply with regulations in the state you are traveling to! Example: You head for the BWCA of Minnesota with your ten foot solo boat. No license, right? In South Dakota, you would be right. But Minnesota requires licensing of all boats over 9 feet! You've got to get on the state websites and figure it out.

Now, joy of Joys, the fee! Licensing fees for non-motorized boats of any sort were nonexistent when some of us started boating. They were just a few dollars a year when we were younger adults. Fees took a big jump about 15 years ago to $7.00/year. Then about five years ago they went to $10.00. Recently the legislature was looking for more license fee revenue to maintain state roads, so in 2011, license fees went to $12.50/year for non-motorized boats over twelve feet in length. Boo, Hiss! But wait; Double Boo, Hiss! As of July 1, 2011, the State, in its infinite wisdom, rescinded the long-standing deal that encouraged boaters to license boats 3 years for the price of 2. Now it is a flat $12.50 per year per boat!!! At least the stickers are kind of pretty, right?

The fine for non-compliance is $80.00-per boat-per incident. Hardly seems fair, does it? Honestly, though, we license all our boats that require it even though the likelihood of getting stopped for no license is pretty slim on most of the lakes we paddle. Like buying an annual BHNF pass, and an annual SDGFP Parks pass, it's a case where it is less painful to comply than to reply to a ticket. And it helps maintain more goodwill between boaters and recreation managers.

A little personal aside, the County Treasurers office, where you go to license all your vehicles, trailers and boats, is staffed with really nice folks! They have traditionally been frustrated registering our relatively cheap, non-motorized boats. Newer boaters, who do not know the process, seldom have the right paperwork after buying a boat and registering it for the first time. But the County Treasurers office staff takes it all in stride! Please reward their patience with the laws they didn't pass by being nice to them! If you think the fee is too much for a boat that will never touch a public road unless it falls off the roof of your vehicle, talk to your legislator, not the clerk in the Treasurer's office!

When you do go to the Treasurer's office to register/license your boat as a new owner be sure to get and bring your Manufacturers Statement of Origin for each new boat. A surprising number of boat dealers do not know about these. Each new boat should come with one. If it isn't there or the dealer doesn't know, there are blank forms you can fill out and swear to. Be sure you also have the boat serial number and documentation of purchase price and date of purchase. No, just your sales receipt will not be enough for all of this. A good bill of sale will work for buying a used boat. Don't dilly-dally too long, though. There are hefty fines attached if you don't register your boat within 30 days of DATED purchase.

Regarding boat serial numbers: Yes, you have one unless your boat is truly homebuilt. All manufactured boats do! You may have to hunt for it, even use a flashlight and magnifying glass. Hopefully it will be stenciled into the hull close to the bow or stern. Look carefully it might be hard to find but it will be there.

The next page is a copy of the SD Boat Title Registration Application, FYI. Understand it is a one-size fits all application. You can see how little of it applies to us as paddlers. Confusing? You bet!

Relicensing boats is simple. All you need is the little reminder card the state sends out a few months prior to expiration, just like for vehicles and trailers. Pop a check in the mail and you're done.

Another quirk of licensing canoes and kayaks: When you register any boat, like your over twelve foot non-motorized canoe or kayak, the Treasurer's office will issue you a Boat Hull Identification Number. This number will also be on your paper registration card so you won't lose it. South Dakota law says every boat requiring a hull ID number must buy minimum three-inch waterproof stick-on numbers and fasten the hull number to the bow of the boat on either side. The license sticker goes behind the hull number; unless your boat is a non-motorized canoe or kayak that is between twelve and nineteen feet in length! Then you will still be issued a hull ID number, but you do not have to paste those ugly hull numbers on your beautiful composition sea kayak or canoe! You just have to display the license decals on each side of the bow. Honestly, we think these license stickers are rather good looking. Of course, if you ever plan on using any motor on your boat then you better stick the numbers on. Black Hills Paddler Kelly's beautiful eighteen foot Kevlar We-no-na Jensen has these reflective orange hull numbers on it because he "might" put a little kicker motor on it with a transom adaptor.

Finally, you are expected to carry the paper registration for your boat in the boat or with you. As boaters who are hard on their boats, we have never found a way to keep a small piece of paper in the boat, and waterproof. After trashing or losing them for years, Most of us have given up and keep boat registrations in the glove compartment or a file at home. After all, you have ID with you (usually) and the boat is licensed. They can come and check if they want...

SHELBY & CUJO ENJOYING PACTOLA

SOUTH DAKOTA BOAT TITLE AND REGISTRATION APPLICATION
See instructions and fees on reverse side

DATE **PLEASE PRINT** MARGINAL WORD

This application is for (Check Only One)

- Transfer
- New
- Out-of-State
- Interstate
- Abandoned
- Operation by Law
- Repossession
- Title Only

Fee ID

SD BOAT (TITLE NUMBER)

Reg. Yr.

DECAL NUMBER ASSIGNED

Reg. Co. No.

NOTE: If applying for a "Title Only"; in signing this application, you are attesting that this boat will not be used upon the waters of this state, or any state.

1-4 Owner's/Lessor's Name: (Last, First, Middle); **Description of type of ownership** (and/or DBA, WROS, Guardianship, Lessee, Lessor, etc.); **Identification Number** (SD Dr. License or SS No.)

1. Owner/Lessor & Lessee — Type of Ownership — SD Driver's License No. or Social Security No.
2. Owner/Lessor & Lessee — Type of Ownership — SD Driver's License No. or Social Security No.
3. Owner/Lessor & Lessee — Type of Ownership — SD Driver's License No. or Social Security No.
4. Owner/Lessor & Lessee — Type of Ownership — SD Driver's License No. or Social Security No.

Title Co. No. — ADDRESS — CITY — STATE — ZIP

BOAT HULL IDENTIFICATION NUMBER

MAKE OF BOAT	YEAR	LENGTH	HULL MATERIAL		TYPE OF BOAT	
		___ FT. ___ IN.	1. WOOD 4. FIBERGLASS 2. ALUMINUM 5. OTHER (SPECIFY) 3. STEEL		1. OPEN 5. OTHER (SPECIFY) 8. SAILBOARDS 2. CABIN 9. PERSONAL WATERCRAFT 3. HOUSE 10. PONTOON (NOT HOUSEBOAT) 4. CANOE 6. INFLATABLE 11. SAILBOAT 7. KAYAK	

BOAT CODE	COLORS	PREVIOUS STATE	PROPULSION	TYPE OF USE
B			1. OUTBOARD 4. SAILBOAT WITH MOTOR 2. INBOARD/OUTBOARD 5. NOT MOTORIZED 3. INBOARD 6. ELECTRIC	1. PLEASURE 2. RENTAL 3. GOVERNMENT-OWNED 4. OTHER

Dealer Price Certification: I hereby certify that the purchase price and trade-in allowance shown on this application is correct.

Dealer Name and Signature of Dealer or Dealer's Agent

1. Purchase Price (see reverse side) .... $ _____
   Bill-of-Sale Not Available _____
2. Less Trade-In Allowance _____ $ _____
3. Difference .... $ _____
4. Tax 3% of Line 3 .... $ _____
5. Credit for Tax Paid to Another State .... $ _____
6. Title Fee and Penalty Fee .... $ _____
7. License Fee .... $ _____
8. Balance Due .... $ _____

Purchased from _____ Name

Address — City — State — Zip

Trade-In

Year — Make — Hull ID Number — S.D. Title No.

IMPORTANT: Original title will be mailed to the owner unless otherwise indicated.

CHECK ONE: Mail to Lienholder   Mail to Owner

PENALTY: Any person failing to pay the full amount of excise tax is subject to a Class 1 Misdemeanor.

☐ **TAX-EXEMPT (If claiming exemption, list exemption # from Section I on back of form.)**

1st Lienholder _____
Mailing Address _____
City _____ State _____ Zip _____

The applicant, under the penalties of law and as rightful owner of the boat described on this application, declares that the information set forth on this application is true and correct.

2nd Lienholder _____
Mailing Address _____
City _____ State _____ Zip _____

Note any additional liens on reverse side.

APPLICATION MUST BE DATED WHEN SIGNED. If boat is co-owned, all owners must sign. If boat is company-owned, company name and title of authorized agent signing the application must be noted.

X _____ Signature ___ / ___ / ___ Date

X _____ Signature ___ / ___ / ___ Date

MV-607-(JUNE 99)

PENALTY: Any person who intentionally falsifies information on the certificate is guilty of a Class 6 Felony.

"You Know You're a Boater When ..."

1 - Your spouse has to park in the driveway because your garage is crammed with boats and paddle gear.

2 - You jump up and try to trace a route through every river and lake you see on PBS nature shows.

3 - Distracted Driver to you means trying not to veer wildly while crossing bridges or driving along shorelines as you look for boaters or paddle-able water.

4 - You love winter only because snow is just water waiting to be paddled.

5 - From March to October your car has that unique blend of neoprene, damp Gore-Tex, and sweat, best described as River Funk.

6 - All your "sick days" last year suspiciously matched the high water days on your favorite water trail.

7 - All your non-paddling friends roll their eyes when the words boat or kayak or paddle are mentioned anywhere near you.

8 - The local boat retailer hands out your personal card to prospective boaters

9 - Your homepage is set to waterwatch.gov and refreshes every 5 minutes.

10 - You drive a $500 car with a $600 roof rack and $5000 worth of boats and gear on it.

Dan and Todd, We got some. The circle is complete.
Rest in Peace Brothers.

GLOSSARY OF "BOATER-SPEAK," TERMS USED IN THIS PADDLE GUIDE & ON THE WATER

<u>ACA:</u> American Canoe Association. National canoe and kayak information and certifying organization.

<u>AW:</u> American Whitewater. National affiliate of international organization focusing on whitewater safety. AW maintains an extensive database of detailed beta about most nationally known paddle routes.

<u>Beta or river beta:</u> Rock climbing jargon for essential information about a route. Kayakers have appropriated this term and use it to describe essential information about a section of a river or creek.

<u>BHNF:</u> Black Hills National Forest

<u>Boat:</u> Generic term for a watercraft. In this book it usually means a kayak or canoe.

<u>Boater or paddler:</u> Anyone who operates a human powered watercraft. The term is inclusive of people who paddle whitewater and/or flat water using a sit inside, sit on top, or stand on top watercraft. The boat can be propelled by paddling, rowing or pedaling the watercraft.

<u>Boat Abuse:</u> A term for paddling a very bony section of whitewater where you scrape the side and bottom of your boat frequently. "That's not algae on those rocks, the green and red is plastic from some serious boat abuse."

<u>Booties:</u> Neoprene socks worn on your feet. When left in the back of your car they tend to really contribute to that river funk smell.

<u>Bony:</u> A section of river or creek that has lower flows and when you paddle it you scrape bottom occasionally on rocks, etc. There is a HUGE range between a little bony and very bony!

Boof: In whitewater kayaking, this refers to the raising of the kayak's bow during free fall, while descending a ledge, ducking behind a boulder, or running a waterfall. This technique is used to avoid submerging the bow of the kayak by ensuring it lands flat when it hits the base of the waterfall. The term is an onomatopoeia which mimics the sound that is usually created when the hull of the kayak makes contact with water at the base of the waterfall. Another type of boof is the "rock boof" which is a move that uses a glancing impact with a boulder at the top of a ledge to bounce the boater over a downstream feature, often finished with a mid-air eddy turn. Rock boofs result in sounds both at the top of the drop (the boat impacting rock) and the bottom (the boat belly flopping into the water).

Brace: A corrective paddling stroke used to keep the boat from capsizing. If you're unfamiliar with this stroke and paddle moving water you will quickly be demonstrating a roll or a wet exit.

Carnage: A jovial term to describe what happens when you misread a rapid or miss a roll or brace and elect to practice your wet exit and hold a yard sale in the downstream eddy. Often times this results in you buying a swim beer.

CFSs: Unit to measure stream flow. Stands for cubic feet per second. Some places measure water flow in cubic meters per second (cms)

Chine: The angle where the sides of the boat meet the bottom. Not to be confused with China, which is where all inexpensive rec kayaks are made.

Class I, II, III, IV, V, VI: Rating system for moving water. A high level of expertise is needed to make objective ratings. Ratings are very dependent upon stream flows, changing obstacles, and the boaters' experience.

Cotton: Clothing made of this can be deadly. Cotton wicks moisture into itself and loses all insulation quality!

Creeking: Boater-talk for narrow, rocky whitewater that can be technically difficult, often times on higher gradient streams with flows that are not typically very high.

Divorce Boat: Term of endearment for a tandem kayak or canoe.

Draw stroke: A corrective stroke performed by placing the paddle out in the water parallel to the boat and pulling the blade towards the hull.

Drop: Boater-talk for an elevation change in a stream.

Dry bag: Storage bag with fold up closure. Usually waterproof (until of course you REALLY need it to be!)

Dry top, dry suit: Waterproof jacket or suit with tight neoprene gaskets at the neck, wrists and ankle. This is a necessity to keep you warm and prevent hypothermia when paddling early spring runoff or in the winter months. Sometimes called the sixth essential.

Eddy: When a rock or corner interrupts the flow of a stream this creates a pool or place where water actually flows opposite to its normal direction. This is a safe spot to stop your boat and catch your breath, to rest, or scout ahead. The eddy-line transition between the normal flowing creek and the opposite flowing eddy can be treacherous.

Eddy Flower: A new paddler who is not confident in their boat handling skills in moving whitewater. Less confident paddlers tend to spend a lot of time resting in eddies while more experienced boaters are playing in river features.

Feather angle: Kayak paddle blades are positioned on different planes on the shaft, at an angle relative to one another (typically 30-60 degrees) to confuse novices and prevent wind resistance when swinging the blades forward.

Ferry: Angling the boat to move sideways or upstream against a current. A Hairy Ferry is a ferry with dire consequences if you screw up.

Flotation: A device that takes up space inside boat to displace water when swamped. Closed cell flotation is usually built in on canoes. Sea kayaks have waterproof hatches that serve this purpose. Air-filled float bags add flotation to whitewater kayaks and rec boats.

Flow(s): The volume of water coming down a stream. The USGS maintains an outstanding website with flows of every stream gauging station in the US listed with real time data. Flow is usually measured in cubic feet per second in this country. This is the volume of water coming through a set line across the stream every second!

FSR: Forest Service Road

Groover: The latrine on a multi-day river trip. Name derives from the time when such devices were re-purposed ammunition cans that left a distinctive groove on one's posterior.

Have You Hugged Your Kayak Today?

Gnar: Big, intense, difficult rapids.

Gunwales: The wood, aluminum or vinyl pieces running from bow to stern along the top of the hull of a canoe. Also what novices typically grab if they don't know how to brace. But please, pronounce the term "gunnels."

Hole: - A spot where water tumbles over an obstacle and reverses course upon itself. This can be a great place to surf a wave. This can also be an extremely dangerous place if it is a "keeper" aka a re-circulating hydraulic.

Huck: The act of running a waterfall. Always a good opportunity to showcase your boof and see how well your boat is outfitted.

Invasive species: Non-native plant or animal species that somehow gets introduced to an area without natural controls on it. Boaters need to be especially vigilant cleaning boats and gear between various lakes and streams to prevent the spread of invasive species.

Keel: A raised ridge that runs along the bottom of a boat from end to end to help the boat track straight and add rigidity.

Lake boat: Synonymous with sea kayak, maybe not outfitted as well.

LED: Light Emitting Diode. A revolution in light technology over standard incandescent bulb technology. Often LED flashlights have battery lives of up to 40 hours on a single battery set!

Lilly-dipper: A paddler who takes their time and is not in much of a hurry to get anywhere. Sometimes used in a derogatory manner to describe a weak paddler.

Line: The route to take through a rapid or around an obstacle. Imagine it as a traced line you will paddle.

Low head dam: A barrier across a river or stream designed to alter the flow of the current. Water overflowing the dam drops water off it vertically, almost always creating a dangerous backwash or hydraulic at the base. These are VERY dangerous especially at higher

flows. Many times referred to as drowning machines.

Maytagged: To get stuck in a hole and thrashed about as if in a washing machine.

Navigable water: The legal definition in SD: any watercourse you can paddle through the summer two years out of ten. The practical definition: anything that has enough water to float your boat in. We paddle many more intermittent streams.

<u>Neoprene</u>: Generic name for wet suit material, hydroskin, second skin, etc.

<u>Ocean or sea kayak:</u> Long (12-19 feet) with storage hatches for gear and aggressive keel for tracking straight, often with  retractable or steerable rudder for tracking as well.

<u>Park & play:</u> Parking close to a river feature and paddling a short distance to "play" on a wave or a hole with no shuttle required.

<u>Paddle jacket:</u> A garment used for paddling that is made of water proof fabric. Often these will have Velcro closures at the wrist. These garments are not waterproof under full immersion but are excellent for keeping you warm and dry from splashing water.

<u>PFD:</u> Personal Flotation Device, sometimes erroneously called a life jacket. When paddling a type III PFD required by USCG. It should be worn at all times when on the water!

<u>Play boat:</u> Special whitewater boat designed with minimum possible length (6-8ft) and volume. Boat floats low in the water to allow paddlers a

platform to do amazing tricks in large waves and holes. Not designed for dangerous big water or high waterfalls.

<u>Pogies:</u> Neoprene mittens that Velcro to paddle. Hands slip in and out easily. Very warm!

<u>Point to safety:</u> A term that means the downstream paddler giving

directions to upstream paddlers always points to the safe water, NOT to the obstacle.

Polypro: generic term for non-cotton, non-wool synthetic clothing that wicks moisture from skin. Often worn as an insulating layer under neoprene layers or a dry top.

Pool-drop: Describes the character of a section or "run" of whitewater. Pool-drop denotes alternating rapids and flat-water or slow sections with nice eddies that allow you to catch your breath and gather your gear. The opposite of pool-drop is continuous.

Portage: Derived from the French word for "carry." A fancy name for getting out of the water and carrying boats around an obstacle, strainer, or between lakes.

Pushy: Boater-talk for a stream that has a lot of gradient or is running at high flows close to or outside its banks. When a stream gets "pushy" it typically takes more effort and experience than normal to make your boat go where it is supposed to go when paddling it. The term originates from how the water actually "pushes" your boat downstream and tries to turn it sideways.

Put-in: Agreed upon location to launch your boats.

Recreational ("rec") boat: Generally a wider, medium length, often less expensive boat made of durable plastic and intended for short trips (1-2 days) on flat-water and moderate whitewater (up to easy class III). Usually has a vertical bow and stern to act like a keel for ease of paddling straight.

Rescue gear: Equipment that ranges from a rescue PFD, knife, whistle, throw/tow line, paddle floats, to z-drags and pin kits. This is must have gear in certain conditions. Do NOT carry gear that you don't know how to use!

<u>River left, river right</u>: For consistency, left and right are always treated as if the paddler was facing downstream. Similar to anatomical positioning in medicine.

<u>River Funk</u>: That unique blend of neoprene, damp Gore-Tex, and sweat that graces a boater's vehicle, basement, and garage during whitewater season.

<u>Rocker</u>: Longitudinal curvature in the bow and stern of a boat along the bottom of the hull. A heavily rockered boat will turn easily and track straight only with practice and good technique. Novice paddlers in heavily rockered boats are an endless source of entertainment.

<u>Roll</u>: Refers to the Eskimo roll method of self-rescue where the paddler uses hip action and leverage to right themselves after tipping over. This is a vital skill for advanced whitewater boaters and serious sea kayakers.

<u>Route</u>: Planned path on lake or stream, usually plotted on a map, with planned starting and stopping points.

<u>Run</u>: Boater-talk for a single paddle trip, usually moving water.

<u>Scout</u>: To physically get out of the boat and verify passage or pick a clean line through an obstacle or hidden section of water.

<u>Shuttle</u>: Shuffling vehicles to and from put-in and take-out points on a paddle route.

<u>Shuttle Bunny or Shuttle Sausage</u>: A term of endearment for a non-paddling significant other who is willing to drop you off at the put-in and is waiting at the take-out with a cool frosty beverage.

<u>Side surf</u>: A play move in a hole in which a paddler uses counter balancing forces of downstream current and upstream hydraulic to hold the boat sideways in either a wave or a hole.

Skirt: Cockpit cover for kayak or canoe that keeps out splashed water from waves or drops.

Solo: Paddling one person per boat.

SDGFP: South Dakota Game Fish and Parks

Strainer: Woody peril. An impassible object, usually a fallen tree that blocks a stream or river either fully or partially. Called a strainer because water will go through, but large particulate matter like you and your boat will not. Consider these seriously hazardous to your health, one of the most DEADLY hazards of boating.

Squirt: Boater talk for letting the undertow of a standing wave pull the bow or stern vertical into the hydraulic as the wave spits the boater out.

Surf: Just like in the ocean, riding a wave. In moving water, waves behind obstacles stay in place and create standing waves. Boaters, typically in whitewater boats get on the wave and stay there to "surf."

SUP: Stand Up Paddleboard

Swamp: When the boat fills with water, this may or may not cause a capsize.

Sweep Stroke: A corrective stroke used to turn the boat by reaching out and ahead, and then "sweeping" in a wide arc fore to aft.

Swim: To leave the boat in a capsize or pin. This can be dangerous in bigger or challenging water. Every boater should practice whitewater swimming skills: butt down, feet forward, and arms guiding.

Swim beer: The beverage a rescued swimmer customarily purchases for his rescuer, to show his gratitude and ensure future rescues.

Take-out: Agreed upon location to end your trip.

Tandem: A kayak designed for two people, see also Divorce Boat.

Throwable: Slang for buoy or cushion that can be thrown to a person overboard. A throw able flotation device is required on motorboats and boats over 19 feet.

Throw rope / throw bag: Floating rope in a throw-able bag used for rescue. Since it is difficult to throw a rope to yourself, you better hope your friends carry one too. For that reason they make ideal Christmas gifts for your paddling companions.

Thwart: A cross-brace between the sides of a canoe or the tubes of a raft.

Tracking: The ability of a boat to hold a straight course due to its hull design.

Tumblehome: The cross-section shape of a hull that decreases in width from the waterline to the gunwales.

USFS: United States Forest Service

USGS: United State Geological Survey

Yard Sale: The appearance of the downstream eddies when your gear floats away after a wet exit and swim. A darn good reason to put your name on all your paddling gear.

Wet exit: To slip out of canoe or kayak when capsized, especially important to practice if you wear a skirt. Essential basic safety skill for all boaters.

Whitewater boat: A shorter (4-9 foot) boat with flat horizontal curves at the bow and stern. These boats are typically made of roto-molded plastic There are two hull types rockered displacement hulls and flat planing hulls. These boats are designed to spin and change direction quickly.

Wood: Boater-talk for trees, shrubs or logs partially or completely blocking (straining) the stream.

Wool: Nature's own insulator, even when soaking wet. Once shunned for scratchiness, new technology has softened fibers and wool is resurging.

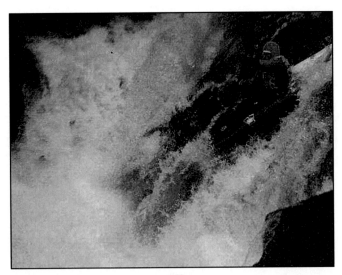

PHOTO CREDITS

A HUGE thank you to everyone who contributed to making this guide a reality. It was a huge collaborative effort only made possible by many people's time and energy. A special thank you to the following people for contributing their photos to the book.

	Page(s)
April Gregory	Cover & 45, 98, 103, 145
Benjamin Ten Eyck	3, 82, 83, 84, 85, 86, 87, 88, 89
Chad Andrew	134, 141
Chuck Liberty	75, 77
Daryl Stisser	108, 110
Dan Crain	111
Cheryl Pruett	102, 113, 149
Jake Anderson	62, 126
Jarett Bies	73, 76, 77, 78
Justin Herreman	20, 42, 43, 44, 46, 58, 63, 64, 65, 69, 70, 71, 74, 101, 106, 128, 131, 154, 156
Kelsey Lane	51
Kelly & Rebecca Lane	15, 16, 17, 18, 23, 24, 25, 26, 27, 28, 29, 30, 31, 32, 34, 35, 36, 38, 39, 40, 43, 48, 49, 50, 51, 52, 53, 54, 56, 65, 75, 112, 114, 117, 152, 157
Kevin Eilbeck	Cover & 47, 93, 97, 104, 105, 107, 153, 157
Lisa Christenson	118
Mike Ray	156
Rick & Julie Emerson	120, 124
Russ Behlings	119, 122
Tim Brumbaugh	115, 123, 153
Todd Andrew	96

ABOUT US

The Black Hills Paddlers are a group of people who love to paddle kayaks, canoes, SUPs, and rafts. We enjoy safe and fun camaraderie while on flat water, whitewater, play-waves, creeks, rivers and sometimes even the snow! We promote water safety for all ages and welcome people of all ages, skill levels, and abilities. Join us on the web at www.blackhillspaddlers.org or on Facebook at www.facebook.com/groups/blackhillspaddlers.

We will see you on the water!

30925284R00095

Made in the USA
Middletown, DE
12 April 2016